ISBN 978-1-330-09739-7
PIBN 10025007

English
Français
Deutsche
Italiano
Español
Português

www.forgottenbooks.com

Mythology Photography **Fiction**
Fishing Christianity **Art** Cooking
Essays Buddhism Freemasonry
Medicine **Biology** Music **Ancient**
Egypt Evolution Carpentry Physics
Dance Geology **Mathematics** Fitness
Shakespeare **Folklore** Yoga Marketing
Confidence Immortality Biographies
Poetry **Psychology** Witchcraft
Electronics Chemistry History **Law**
Accounting **Philosophy** Anthropology
Alchemy Drama Quantum Mechanics
Atheism Sexual Health **Ancient History**
Entrepreneurship Languages Sport
Paleontology Needlework Islam
Metaphysics Investment Archaeology
Parenting Statistics Criminology
Motivational

Christ and Christianity.

THE

STORY OF THE FOUR

(EVANGELISTS).

* *

Christ and Christianity.

THE

STORY OF THE FOUR

(EVANGELISTS)

BY THE

REV. H. R. ⌐HAWEIS, M.A.,

INCUMBENT OF ST. JAMES'S, MARYLEBONE.

AUTHOR OF "MUSIC AND MORALS," "THOUGHTS FOR THE TIMES," "SPEECH IN SEASON," "WINGED WORDS," ETC.

* *

LONDON

CHARLES BURNET & CO.,

9, BUCKINGHAM STREET, STRAND.

1886.

SECOND THOUSAND.

Novello, Ewer & Co.,
Printers,
69 & 70, Dean Street, Soho,
London, W.

FOREWORDS.

CHRIST AND CHRISTIANITY is not polemical, or dogmatic, or doctrinal. It is mainly historical, scenic. It aims at getting as far as may be at the facts—ascertaining what is *certainly*, then what is *probably*, then what is *possibly* true about them. The value of any theories put forth must be tested, as usual, by the number of facts they explain and arrange, and the number of questions they tend to solve. Generally received traditions, such as that Mark was the friend of Peter, and Luke the author of Acts, John the Apostle the writer of the Apocalypse, &c., I have not thought it worth while to question; but no reader can be unaware that weighty authorities are divided in opinion about the exact date and authorship of most of the New Testament writings, so that when I appear to fix such dates and authors, I am only stating what I believe to be the most probable conclusions; selecting and arranging these conclusions as best I can from the heaped-up wisdom of a multitude of counsellors.

I do not set up my own wisdom against theirs, I only claim the right to stand by, read, mark, learn, and choose for myself amongst what are, after all, only various surmises, and sometimes little better than " guesses at truth."

Vol. * * now issued, THE STORY OF THE FOUR, dwells not upon Jesus and the events A.D. 1—33, but rather upon the period A.D. 33—150, which saw them written down. I have here considered the *kind of material* at the disposal of the writers, and commented upon *the use* they have made of it.

The PICTURE OF JESUS (Vol. ✳ ✳ ✳), in *outline* and *colouring*, is in every detail affected by these considerations.

The PICTURE OF PAUL (Vol. ✳ ✳ ✳ ✳) is, of course, far less affected, as both the outline and colouring of his portrait are chiefly provided by the Apostle himself.

The Picture of the Church, from Nero to Constantine, or the CONQUERING CROSS (Vol. ✳ ✳ ✳ ✳ ✳), will bear the impress both of the Master and the bold Disciple who was chiefly instrumental in giving His religion to the world.

But everything pales in importance before the brief divine life of three-and-thirty years, in Galilee. All previous history leads up to it, all subsequent history points back to it, all is either B.C. or A.D.

If I have peered inquiringly once more into that golden mist which hangs over the first century, out of which steps the luminous figure of the God-man; if I have dwelt on the labours of His foremost Disciple, and traced the stages of the Conquering Cross to Constantine, it was only that I might come closer to Jesus Himself as He went in and out amongst men doing good, and understand better the character of His Spirit, and the quality of His work upon earth.

The volume entitled THE LIGHT OF THE NATIONS (Vol. *), which will be issued last, is really the first in order of thought, but like each of its companions it is complete in itself. It contains a bird's-eye view of the Religions of the world, as they appear summed up in the persons of their Founders or in the lives of their Votaries. When their main characteristics are thus held together in suspension—when they are seen for a moment as in one vast mental panorama—

the unity and solidarity of the religious consciousness emerges very strikingly, and we perceive that God has never left Himself without a witness in the heart of man, nor refused to impart a knowledge of Himself to the world, just whenever and wherever and in whatsoever degree the world has been able to entertain it.

It has been well said that the only conception of the moral action of the Divine Being on the human soul, which is *a priori* defensible and philosophical, is a continued and impartial influence, limited to no time, or age, or race, like the great physical forces for ever acting on all particles of matter, yet sometimes resisted, often unseen, but eternally working towards definite ends, Religions, past and present, obey the same law of divine communication, being developed strictly according to the varying measure of human receptivity.

But whilst to "the sundry times past," only one volume has been given, to "these last days," which have to do with the glory of God in the face of Jesus Christ, I have devoted no less than four volumes; and this I apprehend, as Paul would say, is "according to the proportion of Faith."

The aim of these volumes, it will now be seen, is simply to provide a new, and, as far as possible, a true setting for the central figure of Jesus Christ.

I take no credit for original research. Others have laboured, and I have entered into their labours; be it so.

I am merely in the position of a lecturer or professor in class, with the often jarring authorities spread out before him, delivering his free commentary and arriving at his own results.

He professes, indeed, to have read what

has been written upon the matter, to know what has been said; and all he brings with him is a fresh eye, a regard for historical criticism, and, what is as important, a sympathy with the historical imagination, which will help him to combine and re-construct, sometimes from very scanty hints and fragments, an account of the whole matter, capable at least of exciting interest—possibly of bringing conviction.

I have avoided loading my pages with references as a rule, and even used as few texts as possible. Each volume aims at stating results rather than at raising dis-cussions.

Foremost amongst recent contributions to New Testament exegesis, of course, stand Mr. Matthew Arnold's acute books—"God and the Bible," "Literature and Dogma"; Canon Farrar's well digested summaries of learning contained in his " Life of Christ," " Early Days of Christianity," and " Life of St. Paul "; M. Ernest Renan's magnificent contributions to the study of the New Testament—I allude to his six volumes of " Origines "—than which, few more scholarly, and no more poetical and sympathetic pages of local, Oriental colouring, and fine historical imagination, have this century been added to the life and times of Jesus. I need hardly allude to Dean Stanley's, Bishop Lightfoot's, and Bishop Ellicott's masterly and fascinating writings on Palestine and the Pauline Epistles, or Alford's *Greek* Testament ; nor shall I cumber my book with references to such old masters as Neander, Olshausen, Ewald, Strauss, Baur, &c. ; I might just as well print-off catalogues of well-known books, which every one who studies these subjects must consult, and reference to which is usually found in such works as

Smith's "Dictionary of the Bible" and other Encyclopædias. I have naturally drawn freely upon historical manuals, like Mosheim and Milman's "Christianity"; nor have I failed to take account of such clever books as "Supernatural Religion," which have their uses in jolting old-fashioned theologians out of their conventional ruts, but can hardly be considered as excellent substitutes for the Gospel, on the ground of some sharp negative criticism, which, however, does not much affect my general conclusions.

Lastly, I desire to make the frankest general admission of my obligations. I have sometimes followed one, sometimes another writer page after page, adopting here a theory and there a surmise, with a view of arriving at a connected statement, which should aim at carrying with it its own evidence, or such degree of evidence as happens to be attainable. With the effect of any of these statements or re-statements upon current or popular theology, I am no more concerned than a special correspondent at the seat of war is concerned with the effect of his narration upon the opinions or policy of the *Govern-ment* at home. The reporter simply goes out to look on, and to write down. He only wants to know the truth. He is not concerned with bolstering up a policy. Nothing which God has permitted to be true in history can possibly be out of harmony with any other kind of truth, Religious or Scientific. With all the modern appliances of science, historical criticism, geography, philology, and archæo-logical research, any explorer who is so disposed, and has a taste for the work, can now go out into the first three centuries, with his note-book in hand, can look on, and write down.

All that we shall ever know of Jesus is contained in the New Testament, and all that we shall ever know of the New Testament is contained in the writings and the monuments of the first three centuries of the Christian Era. He who can put the monuments and the documents together and read them aright will know all that can be known about CHRIST AND CHRISTIANITY.

H. R. HAWEIS, M.A.,

QUEEN'S HOUSE,

CHEYNE WALK,

1886.   CHELSEA.

CONTENTS.

FOREWORDS . . . . PAGE V

I.

MARK, THE CITIZEN'S STORY.

No.

MARK, THE CITIZEN 3

JERUSALEM AND PELLA.

1. Origins 5
2. A.D. 33 to A.D. 68 6
3. At Jerusalem 7
4. A.D. 66 to A.D. 70 9
5. At Pella 9
6. The events and the Record 11
7. Indifference to written records 12

SOURCES.

8. Oral freshets and written rills 13
9. Modern analogies 15
10. The booklets 17
11. Earliest Gospel fragments 19
12. Golden sayings 20
13. Parable fragments 21
14. Variations 22
15. Papias on Mark 24
16. Conclusions 24

b

CHARACTERISTICS.

No.   PAGE
17. " The " and " A " Son of God 25

18. " The Trinity," 2nd century 26

19. The Carpenter's Son 27

20. No genealogy 28

21. Roman influence 29

22. The very language of Jesus 30

23. Eye-witness memories 31

24. Peter's place in " Mark " 32

25. Mark's pictures 33

26. Peter's impressions 34

27. Mark's theology 35

II.

MATTHEW, THE PUBLICAN'S STORY.

MATTHEW, THE PUBLICAN 39

SOURCES.

28. Matthew in Hebrew 41

29. Matthew in Greek 42

CHARACTERISTICS.

30. Fragments 43

31. Mosaic of verses 45

32. Repetitions 46

33. Genealogies and Childhood of Jesus . . . 48

34. Jewish scruples 51

35. Jewish and Gentile views 53

36. Matthew's Apologetics 54

CHARACTERISTICS—*Continued.*

No.   PAGE

37. Democratic feeling 55

38. Version with a purpose 56

39. Fertile seeds 58

40. A Transition stage 61

41. New wine in old bottles 62

42. It was true. It is true. It is no longer true . 63

43. Perfumes of Galilee 64

III.

LUKE, THE PHYSICIAN'S STORY.

LUKE, THE PHYSICIAN 69

44. Recapitulations 71

DATE.

45. About A.D. 94 ? 71

SOURCES.

46. Paul's Gospel 73

47. Paul's travelling 74

48. Luke and Mark and Paul's parchments . . 75

49. Luke's " eye-witnesses " 76

50. Luke uses Mark, not Matthew 77

51. Summary of Luke's success 78

CHARACTERISTICS.

52. Luke's literary method 79

53. Respect for Roman Authority 80

54. Zealous for Paul's honour 81

55. Running defence of Paul's position . . . 83

56. Partiality to Gentiles 84

57. A Pacific Gospel 85

58. The Eternal and the Transitory 87

IV.

JOHN, THE FISHERMAN'S STORY.

No.   PAGE

JOHN, THE FISHERMAN 93

59. St. John's escape 95

60. St. John at Ephesus 96

61. Men who had seen John 96

62. Tradition about St. John's Gospel . . . 98

63. A Foreigner's mistakes 99

64. More Foreign peculiarities 102

65. Conclusion about St. John's Gospel : . . 103

66. Mr. Matthew Arnold quoted 104

CHARACTERISTICS.

67. Meaning of Gnosticism 106

68. Gnostic Influence 108

69. The Æons 110

70. The λόγος 112

71. The Paraclete 115

72. Memories and Commentaries 116

THE STORY OF THE SHEPHERD AND THE SHEEP.

73. The Good Shepherd Parable 117

74. The Door Parable 119

75. Fidelity and Incoherence 120

V.

LUKE, THE PHYSICIAN'S DIARY.

No.   SCOPE AND COMPASS.   PAGE

76. "We" of the Diary 125

77. The human ever in God 126

78. The Panorama of the Acts 126

AUTHOR AND DATE.

79. Publication why delayed 128

80. Publication why resolved upon 128

81. The Acts in Embryo 129

82. Reticences of Luke 131

CHARACTERISTICS.

83. Luke's Democratic feeling 132

84. Luke a Reconciler 133

85. Good men agreed in heart not head . . . 135

86. The simplicity which is in Jesus 137

87. "Christianity" and "Christ" 137

VI.

JOHN, THE FISHERMAN'S CRYPTO-GRAPH.

THE AGE OF THE APOCALYPSE.

88. Before the Vision 141

89. Special value 141

THE AGE OF THE APOCALYPSE—*Continued.*

No.   PAGE

90. Revelation not before A.D. 68 142

91. Revelation not after A.D. 70 143

92. John the Apostle is the writer 145

93. Why the " Fathers " object to this theory . . 146

94. Revelation no forgery 147

95. John a " Son of Thunder " 148

96. Peculiarities of style and language . . . 150

97. Summary 152

THE SEVEN CHURCHES.

98. Little Apocalypses 152

99. Their tendency to recur 153

100. The Revelation built on Daniel 154

101. The " Angels " of the Churches 155

102. The Seven Epistles—a Jewish and Anti-Pauline

     Manifesto 155

103. Paul's death made a difference 157

104. Jewish Christianity 157

105. The inevitable severance 158

106. Strained relations 159

107. Paul in self-defence 161

108. A bitter application 162

109. Paul on Meats and Marriages 163

110. Paul on Circumcision 165

111. The breach delayed 167

112. The fire breaks out 167

THE SEVEN CHURCHES—*Continued.*

No.   PAGE

113. The survival of the Fittest 169

114. Paul and "the Reformation" 170

115. Two cardinal but mistaken beliefs . . . 171

THE GREAT DRAMA.

116. The Beasts and the Elders 172

117. The strong Angel 173

118. The Book and the Lamb 173

119. An historic retrospect 174

120. The Red Horse 175

121. The Black Horse 176

122. The Pale Horse 176

123. The cry of the Martyrs 177

124. Silence in Heaven 177

125. The Seventh Seal 178

126. The first trumpet 179

127. The false Nero 180

128. The Parthians 181

129. The Temple measured off 182

130. The close again postponed 184

131. The Seven-headed beast 185

132. The Great Cryptograph of Nero . . . 187

133. Thrust in thy Sickle 188

134. The Seven Vials 189

135. The Scarlet Woman and the Beast . . . 190

136 Imperial and Pontifical Rome . . . 192

THE GREAT DRAMA—*Continued.*

No.   PAGE

137. Rome is judged 193

138. Satan is bound 194

139. Gog and Magog 195

140. The Kingdom come at last 196

141. The Crystal River and the Tree of Life . . 198

142. The Spirit and the Bride 198

143. The one Clear Note 199

144. Letter and Spirit 199

145. Immediate impression 200

146. Why Revelation lost ground 201

147. How Revelation regained its place . . . 202

MARK,
THE CITIZEN'S STORY.

B

MARK, THE CITIZEN'S STORY.

No.

Mark, the Citizen.

JERUSALEM AND PELLA.

1. Origins.
2. A.D. 33 to A.D. 68.
3. At Jerusalem.
4. A.D. 66 to A.D. 70.
5. At Pella.
6. The events and the Record.
7. Indifference to written records.

SOURCES.

8. Oral freshets and written rills.
9. Modern analogies.
10. The booklets.
11. Earliest Gospel fragments.
12. Golden sayings.

No.

13. Parable fragments.
14. Variations.
15. Papias on Mark.
16. Conclusions.

CHARACTERISTICS.

17. "The" and "A" Son of God.
18. "The Trinity," 2nd century.
19. The Carpenter's Son.
20. No genealogy.
21. Roman influence.
22. The very language of Jesus.
23. Eye-witness memories.
24. Peter's place in "Mark."
25. Mark's pictures.
26. Peter's impressions.
27. Mark's theology

MARK, THE CITIZEN.

JOHN, *alias* Mark, was essentially a man of towns. In early life he was known as John of Jerusalem; he was at one time a close adherent of Paul, and to the end, notwithstanding their early differences of opinion, he remained in the eyes of that Apostle to the Gentiles profitable to the ministry. Later in life he was known as Mark of Rome, where tradition declares him to have been the near friend and secretary of Peter, the substance of whose teaching is generally admitted to be set down in Mark's Gospel, which was written from memory after Peter's death. Mark's mother, Mary, seems to have been a person in comfortable circumstances. The family lived at Jerusalem, and Mary's house was much frequented by St. Peter and his adherents. It was probably the attraction of Mary's home, with its friendly circle of reformed Jews—its social gatherings and stirring routine of city life—that attracted Mark, the citizen, when he left Paul and Barnabas to plunge by themselves into the wild regions of Pamphylia and Lycaonia. He attached himself to Peter. Peter never had Paul's passion for travelling, though necessity drove him now and again up and down Palestine, and, in all probability, once at least —and once too often—to Rome, where Mark was still his faithful companion. There he may have seen the last of Peter, crucified head downwards; perhaps, too, of Paul — after his second trial before Nero — beheaded outside

B 2

Rome.   He himself disappears, and   makes no sign—
leaving behind him, however, a name associated with the
greatest of the Jewish Apostles, and with the greatest of all
Apostles; and a Gospel—derived from Peter—but not un-
touched with the spirit of Paul.

MARK, THE CITIZEN'S STORY.

___

JERUSALEM AND PELLA.

PEOPLE are eager to hear about the latest excava-
tions at Pompeii and Herculaneum, cities on
the slopes of Vesuvius, which were
destroyed (before the end of Paul's
life) in A.D. 63.

I.
ORIGINS.

The Gospel documents are of more consequence
than Pompeii and Herculaneum.

They, too, have been dug out, in a sense, almost
within the memory of man. History is the field of
their excavation. The ashes of exploded theories—
the lava-streams of controversy and dogma—have,
in times past, submerged the origin of the New
Testament ; indeed, I think they have scarcely
cooled down yet, for the angry subsoil still
smoulders with theological rancour whenever it is
stirred. Still, there is at length a set resolve on
the part of the people to get at what lies beneath

the surface.   The Christian world of the nineteenth century is asking—not what it is possible to
induce people to believe about the Christian records
of the first and second centuries, chief among
which stand the four Gospels—but what is
true.

Now, what is true is, to some extent, *certainly*
known, and may, to some extent, be *probably*
inferred.

We must transport ourselves in imagination to
Jerusalem in the first century; we must follow the
written rills of narrative, then the
oral freshets of tradition wherever we
come upon them; we must take our
divining-rod of sound historical criticism and mark
jealously the spots where the living streams
gush forth; we must follow the direction they
take, until, in a few short years, they are seen
to converge and swell into the Gospel rivers of
Matthew, Mark, Luke, and *John.*

The crucifixion took place about A.D. 33, in
the reign of Tiberius Cæsar—up to that time
there is no trace of a written Gospel.   The Acts
(coming together, 71-2, though issued later) give
a retrospect, from 33 to about 63, when Nero's

2.
A.D. 33 TO
A.D. 68.

monstrous reign was drawing to a close (68). The main points stand out with considerable distinctness. We note the Church's comparative peace—the rise of persecution, the first martyrdom, the first imprisonments, the growing differences between the old Jews and the Judeo-Christians — between the Judeo-Christians, like James of Jerusalem, and the Greek and Roman Christians, like Paul and his followers. *Still there is no written Gospel.*

Paul scours the Mediterranean, from 54 to 67-9, founds his churches in Asia Minor and at Rome, writes his Epistles, and disappears about 68-9. Still there is no written Gospel.

Meanwhile, what was going on at Jerusalem? All the elements of political and religious strife were seething in that vast sectarian cauldron. There were the Jews, who could not agree with each other, and could still less agree with the Romans. There were the Sadducees—the Jewish priesthood was in their hands—rich aristocrats, who hated the people; seeming ritualists, real sceptics—hypocrites. These are the men whom James alludes to as the rich men who oppress the poor and

3.
AT
JERUSALEM.

encourage people with gold rings to take the best seats at church.

There were the Pharisees — the respectable church-going middle-class folk — fond of ceremonies and punctilious in the discharge of religious functions, and neglecting the weightier matters of the law.

There were the Zealots—fanatics—always sighing for the downfall of the Roman Government—thwarting it—threatening it—the very *Commune* of Jerusalem — expecting a Messiah to come shortly in the clouds—disappointed with Jesus on this very account, rejecting Him because His kingdom was not of this world, and " came not with observation."

There were the Brigands, prowling all round the city, bred of the general disorganization of the times — lurking in the suburbs, ready to join any party of action (disorder ?)—with nothing to lose and much to gain by a revolution.

And, lastly, there were the Essenes, Pietists, simple ascetics, dreamers, Ebionites, and lowly followers of Jesus, waiting for the Kingdom of Heaven to be proclaimed upon the postponed but approaching return of their Lord.

It was evident in case of a revolt who would take the lead—the Zealots and Fanatics, backed by the Brigands. They, not the Christians, would form the party of action when the time came.

    4.
    A.D. 66 TO
    A.D. 70.

In 66 the time came. There was a skirmish with the Roman troops under Gessius Florus in the streets of Jerusalem. The Pharisees, the Sadducees, the party of order went to the wall—they lacked the courage to side with the Government. The Zealots and an organised rabble had it all their own way, and even defeated the Roman troops.

In a few months Vespasian, Nero's ablest general, was, of course, advancing through a sea of blood upon the devoted city, and in 70 Titus, his son, destroyed Jerusalem, and the Jews were dispersed never again to reunite—never again to have a country, a city, a temple of their own !

The Christians took no part in these bloody scenes. Quiet, peaceable folk, in no way political, utterly unfit and equally indisposed to be leaders or supporters of a popular revolt, they remembered the words of Christ—they fled to the mountains. Jesus had

    5.
    AT PELLA.

warned them—indeed it required no prophet, even
as far back as 33, to foretell that, sooner or
later, the Communist section in Jerusalem would
come to blows with the Roman authorities. Pilate
had already mingled the blood of some of them
who were Galilæans with their sacrifices, and
the only safety for the Christians would sooner or
later be in flight. Early in 68, when they beheld
"the abomination of desolation"(Matt.xxiv. 15, 16),
the little band of Christians, the relatives and
friends of Jesus, fled to the mountains beyond
Jordan, and settled on the other side of the Peræan
hills, at Pella.

John, probably at this time writing or dictating
at Ephesus, caught the flying rumours of such
events as they floated across the Mediterranean,
and chronicled this first flight of the Christians
to Pella (Rev. xii. 6), " And the woman—*i.e.*, the
Church—fled into the wilderness, where she hath a
place prepared for her of God."

That hurried flight was doubtless little noticed,
so stirring and stormy were the events then
happening in the streets of Jerusalem every
day, yet was it more important than any of them.

That little band of disciples and relations
of Jesus carried with them all that was

remembered of the obscure Nazarene who had flashed into passing notoriety, dazzled the crowd, and then been crucified, and by most forgotten. Fragments of His strange story had indeed survived; *but as yet there was no written Gospel.*

The far-off Pella in 68 was no doubt the land, if not of the written rills, yet surely of the oral freshets which were destined ere long to flow into the four Gospel rivers; *but as yet there is no trace of a written Gospel!*

And this is the first fact to be noted by all who want to understand the various readings, discrepancies, inaccuracies, fragmentary utterances, or even contradictions to be found in the four Gospels, and which not even a rabid orthodoxy can altogether reconcile or ignore. *None of the Gospels were written down until half-a-century after the events recorded in them.* With the recognition of that fact much becomes natural, and, I may add once more, interesting to many readers who may have turned away from the Gospels in despair as long as they were weighted with theories of inspiration out of all harmony with facts or probability.

6.
THE EVENTS
AND THE
RECORD.

We may at first feel surprised that events so momentous as those recorded in the four Gospels

7.

INDIFFERENCE TO WRITTEN RECORDS.

were not sooner written down, but on second thoughts we shall see it could hardly have been otherwise.

Jesus wrote nothing that has been preserved, like the words of Confucius or Socrates — the words of Jesus reach us only at second-hand, generally third and fourth—they have passed, as Mr. Matthew Arnold says, through nearly half-a-century of oral tradition and more than one written account. The first generation of Christians expected daily the return of their Lord. Paul himself, in the Thessalonians (1 Thess. iv. 15) (*cir.* A.D. 52), speaks of his belief that Christ would return during his own lifetime, although at other times later on he seems to have given up that dream, and looked forward to departing and going to Christ instead (Phil. i. 23). To record the past for the sake of the future when the world was coming to an end seemed useless; besides, the bulk of the Christians were poor, most of them probably unlettered and unable to write. And, *lastly,* in those days oral tradition was practised and valued far above written documents. In the

same way, the Vedas existed for centuries un-
written, from mouth to mouth. The Talmud was
only slowly written down, and even then oral
teaching was preferred; and it was so with the
Gospel for some forty years at least after the
death of Christ. Even in 140 A.D., when
many written accounts were current—doubtless,
Matthew, Mark, Luke, and John amongst them
—Papias, a Christian writer, could say, " I did
not consider things from books to be of so much
use as things from the living and abiding voice "
—a sentence which never could have been written
by so eminent a Christian personage had any
such theory of the inspired ànd infallible character
of the written Gospels, such as we are familiar
with, been known or heard of up to 160 A.D.

SOURCES.

Where shall we seek, where shall we find the
Gospel sources ?

The written rills, the oral freshets 8.
of tradition certainly come from the ORAL
FRESHETS
eastern slope of the Peræan hills, AND WRITTEN
from Pella, beyond Jordan, whither RILLS.
the family and the friends of Jesus fled in 68, on
the outbreak of revolution in Jerusalem.

Shall we look once more and for the last time upon the faces of that saintly group—upon the aged mother of our Lord—upon Lazarus, perchance upon Nicodemus, Nathaniel, Joseph of Arimathæa, and the Marys, who ministered unto Jesus in the days of his earthly career?

Some, if not all, of these must have been among the refugees at Pella. Undoubtedly they had the Evangelic tradition—chaste guardians of the sacred relics, second founders of Christianity — and all who wished to know about Jesus would make a pilgrimage to visit these holy personages, around whose heads the aureole was already beginning to gather. Apostles and Evangelists must have been there—remnants of the twelve and of the seventy sent out two and two—and Peter must have paid his farewell visit, previous to his departure for Italy. Matthew may have been there more than once when collecting materials for a Gospel, or perchance the *Logia,* " sayings," of Christ which went by his name. O far off light that forever hangs over those distant Peræan hills ! O heavenly radiance that forever rests upon those saintly faces! O distant voices still echoing down the ages, ye will be forever dear and sacred to all who love the Divine Master !

Truly, as we follow in imagination that little group of obscure Jews, in that lonely mountain village, we can almost see the springs of Evangelic history bubbling up from the virgin soil, a thousand little rills of tradition flowing from those distant hills, until they find their congenial channels, and flow forth to line with their four silver streaks the whole field of future history.

9.
MODERN
ANALOGIES.

In the old days we read how the precious words of Moses passed from mouth to mouth amongst the ancient Jews, and were constantly sown and re-sown in the memory : " Thou shalt teach them diligently to thy children ; thou shalt talk of them when thou sittest in thine house, and when thou walkest by the way, and when thou liest down, and when thou risest up."

The Jewish method never altered, and from mouth to mouth were the words and deeds of Jesus passed by those later Jews—the Christian exiles of Pella. The little forms of oft-repeated words (bunches of sentences) would have a tendency to fix themselves. The most happy and expressive would be apt to suffer but little variation, but no one would be in a hurry to write them down —what is deeply engraved upon the heart need

not be written. We do not write down our
central thoughts for fear of forgetting them ;
but we are ready to repeat them at any time
—" to teach them diligently to the children;
to talk of them when sitting in the house, or
walking by the way, or at nightfall, or at sunrise."

Writing was not so much the fashion in those
days as it is now—no newspapers, no shorthand
reporters, no popular printers and publishers—
the majority of people could neither read nor write,
especially if they were poor, as the Christians
mostly were — fishermen, blind beggars, small
farmers, carpenters, poor women, and some of
more than doubtful character.

Even now how difficult it is to get the actors in
important events to write down their memoirs at
the time. Only twenty years after the American
war does Jefferson Davis (a chief actor) think of
issuing his own account of it, and General Grant's
story comes later still. Scores of eminent persons
with half-a-century of priceless memories die and
leave no line of record. Their oral narrations may
have been frequent and abundant; their words are
gathered up and remembered afterwards; few of
their writings, in some cases none, survive. The
most important events are often those least

remarked at the time. Who knows anything certain about the history of Shakespeare or his plays; or the childhood of William the Conqueror, or Zoroaster, or Æsculapius? And to the outside world, to people like Tacitus, Pliny, or Suetonius; to people like Gallio, Pontius Pilate, Tiberius Cæsar; to the admirers of the beautiful, accomplished, and unscrupulous Berenice; to the gay tourist at Baiæ or Cumæ; to the possessors of villas at Pompeii and Herculaneum; to the street arabs at Rome, who scrawled the still extant figure of a crucified ass on the walls of Cæsar's Palace, and wrote under it *Chrestus;* to the sort of crowds that shouted to see the Christians thrown to the lions in the Colisseum, what was there worth writing about such a people? Their history and their opinions were no more important than those of any gladiator or fanatic, whose prowess or eccentricity afforded an hour's sport or wonder to a frivolous and excitable rabble.

For such-like various reasons no one, either within or without the Christian circle, was in a hurry to write down the floating tales current concerning the eloquent but ill-fated Nazarene who had been crucified

10.
THE
BOOKLETS.

out of Jewish spite; they lived, indeed, from
mouth to mouth, chiefly in the charmed circle.
As one after another Evangelist or Apostle passed
out into the world to teach, he might bear with
him little "forms of sound words"; the oft-repeated
sentences would doubtless get written down in
time, especially when Epistles came to be sent
round—one such fragment, at least, was written
down, a kind of rudimentary Credo, by St. Paul
(1 Cor. xv. 3).

Between the years 66 and 70 there were
probably a great many of these groups of Evangelic
sentences—acts, incidents of Christian life—floating about all over Asia Minor, along the line of
Paul's great missionary voyages. Not a Jewry from
Jerusalem to Rome (and, even before the dispersion of the Jews, little Jewish quarters were to be
found in most Greek and Roman cities) but
would have some bunches of sayings, miracles,
parables, anecdotes, episodes in the life of the
crucified Jew, whose doctrine had already shaken
the old Hebrew orthodoxy to its foundation, and
some of whose followers, especially one Saul of
Tarsus, threatened to confound Jew and Gentile in
a general broad-church *mêlée*, where, according to
this dangerous and unscrupulous person, all class

distinctions should be abolished, and where there was to be neither Jew nor Greek, bond nor free.

Quite suddenly, unexpectedly, we come upon what we are in search of—the earliest fragment of written Evangelic tradition—in St. Paul's Corinthian Epistle (*cir.* A.D. 57). Here, undoubtedly bubbling up from the virgin soil, is one of those written rills. As long as Paul *repeated* it, we had but an oral freshet derived from Barnabas or some aged saint at Pella; but the instant that Paul dictates (1 Cor. xi. 23) the account of the Lord's supper to Stephanas, Fortunatus, Achaicus, or Timotheus, and they write it down, at Ephesus, to be sent to Corinth (A.D. 57), that moment the period of written tradition has arrived (a fragment of written Gospel exists), and we assist at the momentous meeting or coalition between the oral freshet and the written rill.

One example is as good as a hundred. There lies, glittering like a fragment of ore on the surface of a land rich in the same metal, the earliest extant Evangelic text—" I delivered unto you (orally), That the Lord Jesus the same night

II.
EARLIEST
GOSPEL
FRAGMENTS.

in which He was betrayed took bread : and when He had given thanks," &c.

This was written down in *cir.* A.D. 57, and it re-appears in Mark's collection of fragments— or Gospel—with but little change in 70-4 (Mark xiv. 22). Where Paul got it from, or the exact meaning which he attached to those words "from the Lord," we know not. It was doubtless common property by that time, and Mark doubtless got it from Peter.

We can now go to St. Mark's Gospel—the earliest of the four, as we shall presently see—

12. **GOLDEN SAYINGS.** and almost pick out some at least of the embedded fragments of which it is composed. They are set roughly, without the amplification of Matthew, and without the literary art of Luke; but they are the freshest, the *simplest*, the most authentic of their kind. The groups of incidents as they stand can scarcely be improved for the direct force of the eye-witness and rather bald narration. They deal mostly with moments so solemn and so startling that the brain in each case has conjured up the picture. Every motion and word must have arisen before those who heard from the lips of James or Peter, or even of Paul (not himself an eye-witness), the salient features of the last supper —which do not greatly vary—in the Synoptics; or the incidents of the Passion, of which Mark gives naturally the simplest, briefest, and best account, "And they came to a place which is named Gethsemane," &c. Or again, such golden fragments as " They brought young children to Christ," &c. Whencesoever originally derived, it must have been early committed to memory. Irresistibly attractive to all mothers, delightful to repeat, popular with young catechumens, so easy to remember, so tender and so poetical, that its hold over the imagination and the affections is, perhaps, only equalled by that great general invitation — not confined to little children — "Come unto Me, all ye that labour and are heavy laden, and I will give you rest."

The parable fragments, and sometimes groups of parables, stand out no less distinctly to the eye of the historian, if he will only take his stand in Rome or Jerusalem or Pella in the year 70, instead of in the Jerusalem Chamber with the revisers of the New Testament in the nineteenth

13.
PARABLE
FRAGMENTS.

century. The parables are generally disjointed,
occasionally grouped, sometimes, especially in
St. Luke, capping or preceding appropriate events;
in Mark, more naturally set roughly in the text,
with the usual unliterary and makeshifty "And
he said," by way of preface. The little black P's
in our Bible, marking still the old paragraphs, are
often very fair indices of the probable fragments,
or batches of fragments, thus loosely placed—
parables of the kingdom of Heaven, of the sower,
of the wicked husbandman, &c.

In the same way we may pick out the groups of
miracles, healing, casting-out of devils, loaves
    14.   and fishes ; or groups of moral say-
VARIATIONS. ings, floating seeds of divine wisdom
specially calculated to take root in the soil
of an honest and good heart; short, easy
to remember, good to set agoing discourse,
controversy, and that kind of endless pious
commentary dear to the Jews—only too eagerly
learned and ruthlessly practised by the later
Greek doctors at Alexandria; "Salt is good,"
"Judge not," "Love your enemies," and longer
paradoxical precepts, some occurring in Mark
with explanations and in Matthew without;

others occurring in Matthew with explanations and in Mark without; for instance, Mark has this—"How hardly shall they that have riches enter into the kingdom of God!" and adds the explanatory gloss—"How hardly shall they that *trust* in riches!" which is left out by Matthew. Whilst Mark has the sentence about our receiving what we ask for in prayer without qualification—Matthew explains that it is the gift of the Holy Spirit that we may expect to receive, whatever we pray for.

At once we see that dislocated fragments of the same, or similar, utterances have been in the hands of the different compilers, sometimes with a context, sometimes without; that selections more or less appropriate and juxtapositions more or less perplexing or felicitous have been made, according to the method, opportunity, capacity, or even literary taste, or absence of literary taste, in the sacred compiler.

What has now been said applies to the general sources of all four Gospels, especially the first three or Synoptical. It remains to fix "Mark" as the earliest extant written Gospel, and to point out some of its salient characteristics.

Mark was admittedly the companion and inter-

preter of St. Peter, and from this point we are,
of course, more or less upon the
ground of inference, but inference
countenanced by historical and reliable documents.

This is what Papias (140 A.D.) says about
St. Peter, St. Mark, and a record drawn up by St.
Mark, which, in view of continuous tradition,
and in the absence of any evidence to the
contrary, we may fairly assume to be substantially
what has come down to us as the Gospel of Mark.

Papias (quoted by Eusebius) *loquitur :* " This
also John the Elder said : Mark being interpreter
of Peter, wrote down exactly whatever things *he
remembered*, but yet not in the order in which
Christ either spoke or did them, for he was neither
a hearer nor a follower of the Lord, but he was
afterwards, as I (Papias) said, a follower of Peter."

The author of St. Mark's Gospel was, then,
St. Mark. St. Mark interpreted into Greek what
Peter had to preach, and St. Mark
wrote his Gospel in Greek; but when
did he write it, and where ?

Probably at Rome, possibly at Alexandria, and
about 70 to 74. How so ? Peter disappears 64-70.

The Gospel was not written during that Apostle's lifetime, or Papias would not have said that it was written by Mark from *memory;* we may infer then, with probability, that as Peter disappears between 64 and 70, St. Mark wrote down his recollections from 70 to 74. This is inference, but it is fair inference derived from the statement made by Papias embodying the current belief and traditions prevalent in 140 A.D. Any amount of information about Napoleon or Beethoven is believed on similar evidence in the year 1886, although it happened in 1816—about the distance Papias happened to be from the facts which he recorded.

CHARACTERISTICS.

St. Mark's narrative or compilation is therefore Peter's Gospel, and Peter, the most liberal of Judaic Christians, remained to the end Judaic—that is, he retained the Jewish way of thinking about Jesus as the Jewish Messiah or Christ rather than the world's Saviour.

In Mark there is no attempt to define the Divine nature of Christ. Jesus is the Messiah—the Elect of God—the Christ ; never the Son of God—only once (Mark i. 1) "a Son of God"; four times "the Son of Man."

In the first verse of St. Mark our translators have deliberately falsified the text by translating υἱοῦ τοῦ Θεοῦ, "*the* Son of," instead of "a Son"; and the translators of the new Revised Version have been too much afraid of the Unitarians to correct it.

St. Peter's account of his confession stands simply, "Thou art the Christ." Matthew adds for him, "the Son of the living God," &c. One may well believe that Mark's account of Peter's words is the correct one. The Jewish Christians, such as those Apostles, "who seemed to be pillars" at Jerusalem, would naturally not use any language which tended to elevate Jesus to anything above or distinct from their own Messiah, whom they believed Him to be—this was the realisation of their national dream. His approaching return would crown their utmost hopes.

Another theology, the Hellenic, the Pauline, destined to expand when the Judaic or Petrine 18. "THE TRINITY," 2ND CENTURY. had died of inanition in the next century, was in existence, the later Gospels already have it. In Luke,

a Son of God is habitually *the* Son of God;
for Luke wrote after Paul, and Paul had already
preached *the* Son of God, and provided material
for a kind of theological definition *unknown* to
Mark, *unintelligible* to Peter, who found many
things in brother Paul's Epistles hard to understand. By the middle of the second century a
new meaning was current in connection with the
Son of God, who was called the second Divine
Person, and the doctrine of the Trinity was for
the first time announced by Theophilus of Antioch.
" The Christian church," says Mosheim, the
historian, "is very little obliged to him for his
invention. The use of such unscriptural terms
has wounded charity and peace."

But Mark was still in that happy atmosphere—
that world of direct memories and vivid incidents,
in daily converse with one of the
chief actors—where the life of Jesus
made speculation about His person
irrelevant—and the emotion of love and wonder
rendered analysis and definition impossible.

19.
THE
CARPENTER'S
SON.

Forty years and more had elapsed, and men had
hardly begun to enquire where Jesus had come
from, and what had been His early history. What

seemed evident and important was alone the
subject-matter of Peter's discourse—and that was
naturally the *public life* of our Lord, especially His
acts. In Mark we come upon Him for the first
time *full grown,* applying to John for baptism.
Nothing at first seems to have been generally
heard or known of His origin. He was a carpenter's son—few knew more. If Peter knew more,
or attached any importance to what he had heard,
he kept it to himself.

In Mark there is no genealogy—no miraculous
conception — no childhood. As yet the thirty

20.   years before the public ministry lay

NO   in shadow — indeed, we daily see

GENEALOGY.   how difficult it is to recover even a
few meagre and doubtful anecdotes of persons, however famous afterwards, who have been
born of obscure parents and have lived many
years in obscurity; and such was the case with
our Lord. Even His mother plays a very dim part ·
in Mark's narrative—hers was a figure which was
to grow in importance as the years went on, and
her Divine Son's person and mission got robbed of
their human significance and tenderness; but in
the whole of Mark she is not once mentioned by

name, and only once incidentally, as coming to Him and desiring to speak with Him, when He is engaged with crowds of eager listeners. "Thy mother and brethren are without, and desire to speak with Thee," and He looked round about on them which sat about Him, and said, "Behold My mother and My brethren, for whosoever shall do the will of *God*, the same is My brother, My sister, and My mother." Words full of prophecy and radiant with eternal truth. In the spiritual order, as Renan finely observes, birth and heredity count for nothing—the spiritual is all in all—the amount of truth you discover, the good you realise, alone place you—they are the true heirs of Jesus who do the will of the Heavenly Father, who hear the word of God and keep it.

Although Petrine, and to some extent Jewish, in tone, Mark wrote in Greek, and for Gentiles— he is careful to explain what no native of Palestine would require to be told—that Jordan is a river, that

21.
ROMAN
INFLUENCE.

the Pharisees used to fast, that to eat with "defiled" means "unwashen hands," and that at the Passover unleavened bread was used.

Writing at the seat of the Roman Government,

Mark is careful to be courteous and just to the Roman executive. He is very fair to Pilate, indulgent to the Roman officials, respectful to Cæsar, with a leaning towards Syro-Phœnicians, and a glimpse of a wider world than his master, Peter, ever quite took in, though Peter knew more about that world than James.

Mark brings us closer to the Son of Man than any other Evangelist; with him we listen to more of Christ's very words, **22.** **THE VERY** in the original Aramaic, hardly any **LANGUAGE** of which are preserved by Matthew **OF JESUS.** and Luke, and none by John. The dialect is the Syro-Chaldaic or Aramaic Hebrew spoken by our Lord. "Ephatha"—we repeat after Him, and hear Him sigh as the slow process of curing the blind man takes place. "Talitha Koumi." "Maiden, I say unto thee, arise!" We see Him take the young girl's hand, and with the warm human contact we note the return of consciousness out of the deathly trance. We listen to the words which must have fallen thrice upon the drowsy ear of Peter in the shades of Gethsemane—"Abba! Father, let this cup pass from Me." We have preserved the very cry which rang from the Cross and startled into sudden trust even the Roman centurion—"Eloi, Eloi, lama sabachthani?"

But at each step an eye-witness seems to take us by the hand; as Peter went over the events in his memory with Mark, so Mark goes over the same ground with us. In some cases he may even have been an eye-witness himself; everywhere there is the firm, vigorous touch of one who is describing the scene before him—nothing sounds vague— nothing is left to the imagination; in places he is even a little too dry and curt and matter-of-fact. We wonder that the narrative should be so completely unrounded, but the gain in directness and simplicity is immense. The word "straightway" occurs no less than forty-one times. Incidents of no importance are mentioned simply because they happened to have occurred and caught Peter's eye at the time. Thus the blind man appears to have cast away his cloak when he rose and came to Jesus. The swine into which the devils went were feeding under the brow of a hill. The madman of Gadara took up stones to wound himself with. One Simon of Cyrene had

23.
EYE-WITNESS
MEMORIES.

just come up from the country when he was impressed by the soldiers to help to bear the cross-bar of Jesus' instrument of torture, and that other Simon Peter happened to know something of the man, perhaps because he was a namesake; they may have been companions in the country, and one may have been sometimes mistaken for the other, as is commonly the case with Smith in these days. This Simon was distinguished as the father of Alexander and Rufus, about whom we know just so much and no more, but the distinction, Simon of Cyrene, may have been an important one to Peter, as it would be to any man who had a namesake in his village.

No casual reader can miss the significant and impressive place which Peter occupies in his own (Mark's) Gospel. There, as 24. PETER'S PLACE IN "MARK." elsewhere and ever afterwards, he heads the list of the Apostles. There he is singled out, with James and John, to be especially the Lord's companion; there, too, his rash impulsiveness, his courage, his presumption, his cowardice, his misplaced confidence in himself, the scathing rebuke which he received, the denial, the betrayal, " the following afar off," the late repentance and tears, the tender and delicate intimation of pardon from the lips angelic, " Go, tell His disciples and *Peter* He goeth before you into Galilee." These are priceless touches. We feel that not one of them could the listening Mark afford to lose.

Mark is more engaged with the acts than with the discourses of our Lord. Why? Perhaps because the events struck Peter's mind forcibly, but, being an uneducated man, his account of words and speeches was somewhat imperfect; his memory for anything like a sustained sermon was not good. But the life of love was all in all to him. *That* he could not help remembering. One act of mercy and pity and wonder is set down after another, until Mark's sacred gallery is hung with vivid pictures, unconnected, indeed, with each other, but all marked by the central presence of the same Divine Figure, who went in and out amongst men doing good. Now it is the synagogue thronged with eager faces, but the sermon has been forgotten; or a house in Capernaum besieged by an impatient crowd outside; a poor creature, who could not be got

25.
MARK'S
PICTURES.

D

in at the door, suddenly let down in the midst
of the astonished assembly, through the mud roof.
Or it is sunset, after the heat of the day, in
the sudden twilight, with the last red streak
dying out of the sky, the sick are brought on mats
and laid about in the open streets and bazaars,
and the work of healing is prolonged by the glare
of torches or the dazzling light of the Syrian
moon far into the night.   It is ever the sweet and
tender nature of the Son of Man which impresses
Peter, the rugged fisherman, and which is held
up before us. The good Physician, who confined
not His attention to the soul, but ministered
also to the body; the kind Jewish Rabbi, who
had a word of sympathy even for the Gentile
woman; a friendly greeting for the outcasts of
the city, and a healing touch for the lepers.

Ay, and Peter was touched, too, sympathetically
by his Master's feelings; he watched His looks,
he caught the ebb and flow of His
divine emotions. And Mark has set
it all down for us. He has told us
how the beloved Teacher's eye flashed with *anger*
upon those who would have interfered with
the cure of palsied men, how He *sighed* deeply over

26.
PETER'S
IMPRESSIONS

the stupidity and insensibility of His hearers, and at once set to work with some still more simple parable; how He could not bear to see any one suffer without hastening to their relief, and how He was moved with *compassion* when He saw the poor people dropping by the wayside with hunger and fatigue.

Who as he reads might not well lift up his eyes to heaven, and say: "So would I have seen my Lord, so would I have marked the mercy posts of His earthly career, so would I have beheld Him sigh and weep, and work and suffer, and pray for man, so may I even now listen to the words of Him who spake as never man spake, as they drop from the lips of the aged Peter, and are recorded for me by John Mark, his faithful interpreter and friend?" Too brief, but infinitely precious is that record—Mark, earliest and most undogmatic of Gospels, yet containing all that it is vital for us to know about christianity.

No dogma yet, no definition yet, but the love of God and the love of man, the two golden precepts.

27.

MARK'S THEOLOGY.

God, the God of the living, is to us the hope that is full of immortality.

Communion possible with God.

The eternal cry of His children, "Abba! Father."

Belief in the Divine sympathy fixed, immovable.

God cares for and loves the world.

In Heaven indignation and hatred flash out against all evil and badness of heart.

Something yonder in the dim unknown, unseen, yet felt o'ershadowing us, is moved with compassion; appears (or is "manifested") in Jesus, well-beloved Son of God—into whose Kingdom we are all called, and in whose name we are all baptized.

These truths are won, the world will not let them go. They are all enshrined in the earliest Canonical Gospel, the Gospel according to St. Mark.

II.

MATTHEW,
THE PUBLICAN'S STORY.

MATTHEW, THE PUBLICAN'S STORY.

No.

Matthew, the Publican.

SOURCES.

28. Matthew in Hebrew.
29. Matthew in Greek.

CHARACTERISTICS.

30. Fragments.
31. Mosaic of verses.
32. Repetitions.
33. Genealogies and Childhood of Jesus.

No

34. Jewish scruples
35. Jewish and Gentile views.
36. Matthew's Apologetics.
37. Democratic feeling.
38. Version with a purpose.
39. Fertile seeds.
40. A Transition stage.
41. New wine in old bottles.
42. It was true. It is true. It is no
    longer true.
43. Perfumes of Galilee

MATTHEW, THE PUBLICAN.

MATTHEW was a " Portitor." The Roman taxes being
usually in the hands of Roman knights, these high
personages farmed the Customs out to local men, " Porti-
tores," who, having to pay a fixed sum for the privilege
of collecting, squeezed as much in addition as they could
out of the people. The police winked at the extortion ;
there was seldom any redress, but the " Portitor," or
collector, was generally hated. He was employed by the
knight much as the hangman is employed by the Sheriff,
to do the dirty work. His prey were the rich and middle
classes—out of the dregs of the people he could not raise
very much. He was glad, probably, at times to take refuge
with them, and they would be flattered by the attentions
of a richer man, however looked askance at by his social
equals. At any rate, Matthew had a certain following
amongst the lower orders, and a good many of them rose
up and followed him when he rose up from the receipt of
Custom and followed Christ. What became of him afterwards we can but vaguely conjecture. To the end, if we
are to judge by a certain bias in the Gospel which bears
his name, he remained a Jew, with a double conscience—
full of Jewish ardour, respect for the Temple, attentive to
ceremony, though disliking the Pharisees—indeed, they
may have suffered from his exactions, and reciprocated his
hatred—wholly changed in heart, he was but half changed

in mind. He records with reverence many sayings which must have remained strange and unintelligible to him. Although writing or editing after Paul's death, he probably had no idea of Paul's importance. To him Christianity is still the work of the twelve. He is the type of the transition period between Judaism and Christianity, and his value lies wholly in his memory and the abundance of *Logia* which early passed current under his name and have found a place in the Gospel which is sealed by it. We shall associate Matthew of Capernaum, in Galilee, most correctly with the inner circle at Jerusalem—the friends and family of Jesus. He may have left the doomed city in their company, and taken refuge with the saintly little group in Pella, beyond Jordan. There, in converse with the mother of Jesus, who kept so many sayings in her heart, with Nicodemus and Cleophas and Nathaniel, and now and then one or more of the twelve, Matthew may have collected sundry "libelli," or booklets, and formed a record supplemented from his own memory. Living mostly with Jews, he would recognise in Jesus the Jewish Messiah, and lay special stress on that; but the value of the Gospel is not in its theory, which is ill-defined, or its incident, which is largely derived from Mark, but in its words—they are spirit and they are life— they inspire the real Gospel according to Matthew.

II.

MATTHEW,
THE PUBLICAN'S STORY.

SOURCES.

MARK, then, is the earliest of the four extant Gospels, the first of the Synoptics, and its source is Peter, and its author is John Mark, and it was written in Greek, at Rome, after Peter's death, about 70—75.

28.

MATTHEW IN HEBREW.

But there seems to have been a still earlier Hebrew Gospel current in Palestine. It may have been compiled by the refugees at Pella, and consisted of oral traditions, including, perhaps, an important batch of sentences and fragmentary discourses of our Lord, known as the *Logia* of Matthew. This early Gospel was quoted, but quoted in Greek, by Clemens Alexandrinus, A.D. 217; Origen, A.D. 253; Eusebius, A.D. 340; and Jerome, A.D. 420. It disappeared in the fifth century with the destruction of the Judeo-Christians of Syria.

We cannot safely make up the Gospel of
Matthew without reference to this Hebrew Gospel

29. and the *Logia* which passed under the
MATTHEW IN name of Matthew. Our Gospel of
GREEK. Matthew seems to have arisen thus:—
Mark's Greek Gospel, 70—5, may have reached
the East about 80, and its extreme meagreness
must have immediately struck those who had
many more ample traditions—had, in fact, the
Hebrew fragments of the *Logia*, or speeches of
our Lord, in their hands.   Mark reports Christ's
sayings very briefly and imperfectly.   The *Logia*
and the Hebrew Gospel reported them much
more fully; but Mark's narrative, coming from
Peter, was very authoritative and precise, especially for the acts and incidents of Christ's
life. The obvious compilation and completion
now takes place. Between 80—90 the Syrian
compiler sets to work upon a new Gospel, his
materials being Mark, *Logia* of Matthew, and any
current oral and written traditions extant in
Pella, Batane, or Kokaba, amongst the few sur-
viving friends and relations of Jesus.   There were,
as we learn from Luke, many current accounts.
The Gospel gets its stamp from the *Logia* of
Matthew, and the compiler, following the common

practice of the time, affixes Matthew's name
to the compilation; indeed, all that is most
characteristic about it, all that distinguishes it
from Mark, may well be Matthew's own, although
Matthew was probably dead when the compiler
used up his *Logia* in the Gospel which now bears
his name.

The Gospel now called St. Matthew's was,
then, written in Greek (or it may have been the
original Hebrew Gospel translated) *cir.* A.D. 85, in
Syria, but addressed to Jews. It omits explanations of places and Jewish ceremonies (without
point in Syria), it inserts allusions interesting to
the East (without point at Rome); its written rills
and oral freshets were derived from St. Mark, the
note-books or the memories of Syrian Christians,
and especially the *Logia* of Matthew.

CHARACTERISTICS.

With these general clues we may take up the
Gospel according to St. Matthew as it stands, and
see how it bears witness to the general
probability of what must after all be,   30.
                                       FRAGMENTS.
to some extent, these guesses at truth;
guesses they may be, but such guesses as
are fair inferences from known facts; theories

they may be, but theories which, after all, arrange, explain, and make intelligible many facts better than any other theories—certainly better than the old, worn-out theory of verbal inspiration.

The speeches of our Lord, in Matthew, form a somewhat rough mosaic with the adapted text of Mark. The longest is the Sermon on the Mount. There is no real connection between its various sections, although commentators have, of course, made out one, and far be it from me to quarrel with any reader who is satisfied with their ingenuity—for purposes of edification it may even be commended. The so-called sermon is, in reality, a collection of sayings, sometimes coherent for twelve verses, or four verses, or six verses, the little black P's in the ordinary Bible marking very fairly the unconnected paragraphs. It is not impossible that one or more of these paragraphs, or the sense of them, may have been spoken at the same time; there is no proof of this, nor can there be any proof, and there is no proof to the contrary. Our Lord probably spoke at times for an hour or more, whilst this, His longest so-called Sermon, can be read in less than ten minutes. This is sufficient to show that we are dealing with fragments, headings, texts, rather than sustained utterances, which is obvious enough to anyone not a commentator. In Chapter xxiii. the sum and substance of the bitter things said about the Pharisees is concentrated, but they may have been often repeated in different forms on many separate occasions.

In Matthew you will find many curious repetitions with variations, which can only be accounted for by supposing that two reports of a similar saying have been copied without being combined.

31.

MOSAIC OF VERSES.

Take, for instance, the saying about being a true disciple and taking up the Cross and following Christ—losing one's life to save it, &c. The original passage is in Mark viii. 34, 35—copied very nearly verbatim into Matt. xvi. 24, 25; but in Matt. x. 38, 39 we have repeated a similar sentence in an altered form and in a different connection. The compiler has probably found that utterance not in Mark, but in the *Logia,* or some other collection, and although he keeps the saying as it stands in Mark, he fears to lose something by suppressing it when he comes upon it over again, so down go both versions in his Gospel. Why, we can almost look over his shoulder and see him at work. Absorbed with his *Logia* in the earlier part of the Gospel, the compiler of Matthew inserts the passage as it occurs there (x. 38); later, about the time he has come to the advanced portion of his work marked by the xvi., he has read on to that portion in Mark which stands in Chapter viii., and if in the first place he could not bear to sacrifice his Hebrew-Syriac material and the *Logia*, now he can still less bear to sacrifice his Græco-Roman material or St. Mark, and so both are mosaiced into different parts of the new Gospel according to Matthew.

And this consideration also explains many repetitions of incidents as well as of obscure sayings.

32.
REPETITIONS

Two cures of two blind men, of two deaf mutes, two miracles of loaves and fishes, two demands for a sign, two sentences on divorce, two demoniacs of Gergasa, two disciples of John, two disciples of Jesus. Of course, it is not impossible that two similar events may have occurred, and so got recorded. It is also probable that sometimes the same event has done duty for two, only because it has been twice told independently.

And sometimes the cut looks so fresh that you can almost see the incision made for the insertion— as when in walking in some garden in summer the eye is caught by a graft let into a standard rose tree—the join has never quite closed up, the foreign shoot is quite apparent; it grows there now, but we can see it came from elsewhere, and had another stock.   This is strikingly so with the story of Peter going to meet Christ as He came walking on the sea.   In Mark you have Christ alone walking on the sea, and Matthew (xiv. 28) uses the narrative up to Mark vi. 50, " It is I, be not afraid."   Matthew then inserts (28-31) the story of Peter—strangely enough left out in Peter's own Gospel (Mark)—and resumes Mark's text at 31.   And I might point to many other instances of Matthew's interpolations in Mark's text, such as the piece of money in the fish's mouth; Judas' inquiry, " Is it I ?" Jesus blaming Peter's sword stroke ; Judas' suicide ; Pilate's wife's dream. But we come now to some far more significant interpolations.

Other gaps corresponding to other demands had to be supplied.   In Mark there were no gene- alogies, nothing about the miraculous conception,

the Divine Paternity of Jesus, the anecdotes of
childhood.   Indeed, as I have noticed
in the case of other great characters
in history, so in the case of Jesus,
the future of no child can be foreseen, and when
that child is of obscure parentage, least of all
are the stories of childhood, or the title-deeds
of its descent, likely to be at once forthcoming.
If such are ever recovered, or related, they are
recovered afterwards, and related to a dead
certainty with a purpose.

33.
GENEALOGIES
AND
CHILDHOOD
OF JESUS.

Neither Mark nor Peter in those early days
seem to have troubled themselves much about the
parentage or genealogy of Jesus ; to them His
parents (whatever their remote ancestry may
have been) were obscure, unimportant, and rather
obstructive personages. To the plebeian fisherman
it would not occur, even after he had confessed
Jesus as the Jewish Messiah — the Christ — to
enquire whether His descent could be traced from
David or from Adam ; but that was a question
which would at once pre-occupy a man like
Matthew or Luke, who knew the law and the
Prophets.   A fisherman would be naturally incom-
petent to raise such questions. The genealogies
used by Matthew and Luke are the careful

compilations of some scribe—some cultivated member of the very poorly cultivated Christian community. The early Judeo - Christian line ot thought seems to have been this : to the Jewish Christian, Christ is the Jewish Messiah, therefore of Royal descent. His reputed father being Joseph, Joseph's descent must necessarily be traced to David. It is so traced in Matthew and assumed in Luke. But the interesting point about these genealogies is the early stage of opinion they both record—*i.e.*, the view that Christ was the Son of Joseph. Both Matthew and Luke announce the later stage of opinion as well—*i.e.*, that Jesus was of Divine parentage by the Holy Ghost, in which case, of course, Joseph and his genealogy become alike meaningless.

Both opinions about the birth of Jesus are stated, both being held at different times, but no attempt is made to reconcile them. A very sufficient answer to those who think that the Gospels were late compositions concocted in order to impose upon the world.

Towards the close of the century (nearly a hundred · years after the event), the Divine parentage of Jesus had entirely displaced the earlier belief that He was the son of a carpenter,

but it was still necessary for the sake of the
Jewish Christians to show that, although He
might be more than the Jewish Messiah, because
the Divine King and Saviour of the Gentiles
(which many Jews were loth to admit), He was, at
any rate, the Jewish Messiah too. Later on, the
mistake, from the Divine parentage point of view,
of tracing up from Joseph to David was seen,
and an attempt was then made to save the royal
descent by tracing from Mary, who undoubtedly
was His mother, up to David; but it was
too late. The (entirely irrelevant) genealogy
of Joseph for better for worse had taken its
place as it now stands in the Christian records
and could not be displaced, and the genealogy
of Mary was too recent and too long after the
event to be received at all. It has not been
found possible, as far as I know, to collect
any evidence to show that the account of the
miraculous conception was at all generally current
during the lifetime of the Blessed Virgin; indeed,
it may have been one of the things which she kept
and pondered in her heart, and which, like many
other sacred confidences, rather leak out than are
proclaimed upon the house-tops. The same is
true of the childhood stories. None of them are to

be found in Mark, and only two in Matthew—*viz.,* the Magi, and the massacre at Bethlehem with the flight into Egypt. From this time until the death of those who had seen the eye-witnesses, or about the time the Johannine Gospel closes the four authoritative biographies of Christ, tales of the infancy increased and multiplied, and the doctrine of the Divine parentage, a sad stumbling-block to the (monotheistic) Jew (as Paul hints), established itself just in proportion as Christianity became, through Paul's ascendancy, the religion of the (polytheistic) heathen. But neither genealogy nor the Divine parentage, nor the tales of the childhood, seem to have gained ground until about eighty years after the events related, or about half-a-century after the death of our Lord.

Then, as now, the evidence for the human parentage, such as it was, was in the hands of the Christian Church. Then, as now, the evidence for the Divine parentage was also in the hands of the Christian Church, and in each case the conclusion could not well have been other than what it was. The Gentile Christian was naturally eager to show that the Founder of

34.
JEWISH
SCRUPLES.

his faith claimed to be as divine, or more divine, than any of the gods of the heathen. The Jew was equally anxious to show that he was as monotheistic as ever, in the midst of the Greeks and Romans, his hated masters, and that Jesus was the national Messiah, about to return in the clouds and confound His enemies. Accordingly, when Jesus did not return, Jewish Christianity died; it had nothing left to stand upon; but Gentile Christianity, witnessing to the eternally human side of God in Christ, had eternal truth on its side, though in time it too showed a tendency to outgrow the dogma or special form in which that truth had first been clothed.

The doctrine of the human parentage was probably the only doctrine accepted by the Jewish Christians until about 70—Paul's doctrine not finding favour with the Judaizing Christians. The doctrine of the Divine parentage, which soon became popular with the Gentile followers of St. Paul, was probably one of the causes which brought about the final disruption between Christian and Jew; that, together with the Pauline repudiation of Mosaic rites, fixed the great gulf between them, which has lasted ever since.

When, in the eyes of the Jew, the Christian

had reduced the Deity to a level with the
numerous gods of the surrounding nations, by ascribing to Him a human
relationship, against which the whole

of the national faith, and Jewish history, and
inspired teaching seemed one long protest —
their Messiah, their Christ, appeared by such
teaching to be at once merged in the crowd of
heathen deities, and the old fatal mingling with
the heathen denounced by the Prophets threatened
to recommence (indeed, Jesus was so merged in
the eyes of those who set up a niche for Christ
in the Pantheon). The Divine parentage seemed
to be a slight upon the Jewish monotheism, which
Greek, Alexandrine, or Athanasian metaphysics
alone could deal with, just as the abolition of the
law seemed to be a slight upon Moses, which
no Sermon on the Mount could really explain
away. When these doctrines became, towards
the close of the first century, identified with
Christianity, the severance between Jew and
Christian was, in fact, accomplished, though
old Jewish associations and ritual practices,
such as keeping the Sabbath as well as the Lord's
day, and the widespread use of circumcision, still
lingered on for a century or more.

We note in the later Gospel of Matthew how much stress is laid on pure miracles; the
36. secondary causes dwelt upon in MATTHEW'S Mark, such as anointing with clay APOLOGETICS and taking by the hand, &c., almost disappear in Matthew.

Notice also the apologetic tone. The believers in Christ were already beset with questions. We can almost hear the objections raised as we read the answer provided for them in Matthew. The words and incidents are so arranged in Matthew as to present a bold front of defence to the various counts. Men said, for instance, that John the Baptist had not believed in Jesus, or had ceased to believe. Answer: That Christ had sent back His messenger with overwhelming proofs of His Messiahship.

It was noticed that the very towns in which He had worked most miracles had been most sceptical. Answer: Chorazin and Bethsaida were worse than Sodom and Gomorrah. The fact had not been only noticed by Christ, but commented upon and explained as altogether strange and exceptional. It was said with a sneer that people who understood the law did not admit that Jesus was even the Messiah or Christ. He had very imperfectly filled the position assigned to the Jewish Messiah; He did not come in glory; He did not redeem Israel; He did not crush their foes. Answer : These things were hidden from the wise and learned, and revealed to babes. He was a King and a Conqueror, but His kingdom was not of this world; His triumph was not over a visible foe, but over a ghostly enemy; that enemy was not the Roman Government, but the Devil. The promised signs of Messiah were wanting. Answer : An evil and adulterous generation sought after a sign, and no sign should be given them. The mighty works some had seen and some had believed in were sufficient, as for the others, they would not believe though one rose from the dead.

Throughout Matthew there is the strongest and always most effective appeal to the democratic instincts. Every cause which is to win the ear of the masses must live on such appeals.

37.
DEMOCRATIC
FEELING.

To the objection that the Jewish nation had rejected Him, it was replied—Not at all. Only the upper classes had rejected Him, because He was a poor man, the son of a carpenter, but

even they feared Him, because He was beloved by
the people at large, and the aristocrats dread the
mob. Popular enthusiasm was always dangerous,
especially when excited and ruled by men of the
people, and the people were all on Christ's side.
If He had been sacrificed, it was as a popular
leader, by the haughty Sadducees and Scribes and
the jealous priests, who were in power at the time.
It was all the fault of the Government ! That is
an explanation which always seems satisfactory to
the masses. The Conservatives were then in
power at Jerusalem, and, as usual, they had made
one more blunder, and sacrificed the people's
champion.

The words of Christ might so be arranged as
fully to bear out this view of the whole case. He
38. constantly turned to the people —
VERSION
WITH A "The poor," He said, "were to
PURPOSE. have the Gospel preached to them ";
"Blessed were the poor"; "Blessed were
the persecuted ones"; but as for the rich,
"It was easier for a camel to go through a
needle's eye than for one of their sort to get into
the kingdom of Heaven."
The Pharisees prided themselves upon their

spiritual privileges and upon their social position —they thought they were righteous and despised others. Well, what would be the end of that? Why, the publicans and harlots would go into the kingdom of Heaven before them!

It is easy to see that Mark wrote without after-thought; he put down what he remembered. If it squared with people's ideas well—if not, still there it stands.

But Matthew has already a new version—a case—a cause.

What seems in Mark a little crude, or shocking, or inappropriate, Matthew will almost uncon-sciously tone down or omit.

Mark relates, for instance (iii. 21, 31, 35), how His friends thinking Him mad came upon Him to arrest and bind Him as He was surrounded by an excited crowd; but Matthew, in relating the episode of His mother and brethren standing without and desiring to speak with Him—prepared, no doubt, to put Him under immediate restraint, if they could succeed in getting at Him—omits all reference to their design or to His supposed madness (Matt. xii. 46-50.)

Mark vi. 5, "He could there do no mighty work," is toned down in Matthew xiii. 58 to

" He did not many mighty works there." Mark's
Scribe, who questions Jesus about the commandments, does so in all good faith, but Matthew,
writing in Judæa, finds the Scribes in far too bad
odour with the followers of Jesus to be credited
with common courtesy or fairness, and brings in
the lawyer as "tempting" Jesus with his questions. The "Blessed are the poor," "Blessed are
the hungry," of Mark, had probably given rise to
some discussion and various objections, and so
appear in Matthew with an appropriate or explanatory addition, "The poor *in spirit*," "The
hungry and thirsty *for righteousness*."

Although, in Matthew, we have in a sense got
back from Rome to Judæa, we feel that we are
39.   gradually getting further and further
FERTILE   from the events and scenes related. In
SEEDS.   90, the friends of Jesus are dying daily,
all His immediate relations, including His mother,
have probably disappeared. The outlines of time
and place are really blurred and indefinite, and
with a certain charm and semblance of accuracy
the exact sounding statements in Matthew and
Luke turn out, after all, to be vague—"In that
hour," "At that time," "It came to pass."

And Matthew exhibits probably the first growth of what we may call Gospel Haggada, or edifying gloss literature. It is the very law of such proverbs and parables as those of Jesus that they should increase and multiply—they are far too living and fertile to stand long alone; they are seeds, and already, in Matthew, they have been planted out and begun to germinate.

There never yet was a teacher who had not ascribed to him utterances unuttered by him, which yet were truly his, because the offspring of his spirit in the minds of others. The people create them as pupils paint school pictures. The pupils and disciples speak and think just like the Master; once give them a clue, a method, a specimen, one or two genuine parables beginning—" The Kingdom of Heaven is like this or that," and from such a seed a dozen parables, equally forcible, will spring up; and, though the Master may not have spoken them all, they are still His. He is the real creator. In every art, as in literature, the same process is going on; the law of sympathetic reproduction is uniform. The disciple paints like, or copies, the Master, and after His death the school picture passes for an original. The great composers, the great violin makers, the great poets have had such close followers that good judges are taxed to separate the copy from the prototype ; at times even we detect the master's own work in the copy, or the pupil's work in the original, as when Nicholas Amati makes a violin and leaves a scroll to be cut by his pupil, Stradivarius; or Leonardo paints an angel's head into his master's picture.

And we may fairly assume that in the larger Gospels of Matthew and Luke parables on the model and sayings in the spirit of Jesus' teaching may find a not inappropriate place ; it may not be possible always to separate the seed and its aftergrowth, still, as has been beautifully said, " Jesus is, after all, the Creator—He did all—even what has only been attributed to Him ; Jesus and the work of His spirit are inseparable.   There was in Him what theologians term a communication of idioms.   The speech of many bewrayed them ; it was not difficult to take knowledge of them that they had been with Jesus ; nothing can take out of the Gospels a certain original freshness of narrative and the stamp of a manner caught from the life." It is ever " That which our ears have heard, that which our eyes have seen, that which our hands have handled."

Lastly, Matthew, though compiled, let us say, fifteen or twenty years after Paul's Epistles, reflects an earlier Judaic stage of development. Matthew is still over-shadowed by Moses. He is a Jew, and yet not a Jew. The Gospel moves in the penumbra of the law. Paul abolished all for Christ, and his theology was already abroad, though rejected by those who cared at all for Jewish Christianity, and the compiler of Matthew was certainly among such. Matthew embodies the transition period between the Petrine and the Pauline Christianity, just as Mark embodies the Petrine and Luke the Pauline Christianity.

40.

A TRANSITION STAGE.

Matthew's compilation is the work of a double conscience; between two worlds at that moment Christianity hovered like a star. Matthew is neither Jew nor Christian. He insists on separation from the law, yet clings to the law. The characteristic transitional formula repeated by Christ is "The Ancients said one thing, but I say another." That is the type of the transition. Jerusalem still is "the Holy city," "the Holy place." The kingdom of Heaven is clearly local, and not a hundred miles from Judæa. The Pharisees are hated and denounced, yet their authority is recognised; they sit in Moses' seat and must be obeyed, but not imitated. The law was, and the law was not. Jesus destroyed it, but Jesus fulfilled it too. The Sabbath is suppressed, yet the Sabbath is kept. Jewish ceremonies are observed, yet no stress is laid upon them, and ceremonial payments are even denounced. ("Ye pay tithe of mint," &c., Matthew xxiii. 23).

We are in a land where the moral revolution going on is even greater than the political one.

41. NEW WINE IN OLD BOTTLES. The political revolution destroyed the Jews as a nation, but the moral one created a religion which has lasted with unimpaired, though not unchanged, vitality down to the present time.

The new wine was then still in the old bottles, but it was bursting them; yet the new bottles were not quite ready, and the old bottles had to hold out still for awhile. Transference from the old forms must come, but, if the wine is to be saved, not too suddenly. Terrible moment for eager spirits who saw beyond their age! Time full of bitter recriminations and misunderstandings. Those who would shift the old religion on to the new lines without a bloody revolution bear painfully with the forms of the old religion, and are sure to be denounced by the fanatics as traitors in the camp. *So was Paul;* but the wisdom of the Ancients justifies the patience of those who toil towards the future, bearing on high the dusty banner and wayworn symbols of the past until they rot and crumble in their hands.

On every creed of the past is inscribed in characters visible only to the prophet's eye three sentences—" It was true.   It is true.   It is no longer true." So the Talmud, when it cites opinions mutually destructive, adds: "And all these opinions are the words of life."

42.

IT WAS TRUE.
IT IS TRUE.
IT IS NO
LONGER
TRUE.

The parable is an eternally recurrent one.   All religious reformers are obliged to act as Paul acted when he shaved his head at Cenchrea because he had a vow, or refused to eat meat offered to idols. A burden become intolerable can only be lifted by being borne patiently for awhile, without abatement or reserve.

As was the passage between Judaism and Christianity, so was the passage between Catholic Christianity and Protestant Christianity.   So

must be the passage between Protestant Christianity and the Christianity of the future, which
is even now taking place—Both grow together.
By-and-bye comes the hour to reap, when it is
found that the tares, which it was not safe to pull
up earlier, are already brown and withered, whilst
the good corn stands up in their midst strong and
brave—the new bread of God, fit at last for the
food of man.

"The words that I speak unto you," said Christ,
"they are spirit, and they are life"; and the
"words," the *Logia* of Christ, belong
to Matthew. They have wrecked one
form of Christianity after another. They
have exploded the bad metaphysics of Alexandria,
the scholastic theology, the mediæval superstition,
the dogmatism of Rome, and the counter-dogma-
tism of Protestantism; the affectation of the
Positivist, and the mock humility of the Agnostic.
Those who would know the religion of Christ
must learn the Sermon on the Mount, and the
parables by the Lake. There, and there only,
will be found the true perfumes of Galilee, the
Gospel of the kingdom, ever the same in substance,
ever changing in form; there, and there only, will

43.
PERFUMES
OF GALILEE.

Christ be seen once more transfigured before us—greater than Moses and the Prophets; greater than Peter, James, and John; greater than Paul. Yes, towering above all the churches that take His name in vain is the Christ that spake as never man spake—the Christ of the Gospel according to Matthew.

F

LUKE,
THE PHYSICIAN'S STORY.

F 2

LUKE, THE PHYSICIAN'S STORY.

No

    Luke, the Physician.

44. Recapitulations.

DATE.

45. About A.D. 94?

SOURCES.

46. Paul's Gospel.
47. Paul's travelling.
48. Luke, Mark, and Paul's parchments.
49. Luke's " eye-witnesses."

No.

50. Luke uses Mark, not Matthew.
51. Summary of Luke's success.

CHARACTERISTICS.

52. Luke's literary method.
53. Respect for Roman Authority.
54. Zealous for Paul's honour.
55. Running defence of Paul's position.
56. Partiality to Gentiles.
57. A Pacific Gospel.
58. The eternal and the transitory.

LUKE, THE PHYSICIAN.

A PHYSICIAN indeed, and, like so many physicians, a man of wide sensibility, culture, and intelligence. If an Antiochene, he probably met Paul at Antioch, and seems to have been drawn very close to him about A.D. 52, when the Apostle was recovering from the severe attack of ophthalmia which prostrated him for a time in Galatia. Luke's profession, probably, took him much on board the ships that plied between Troas and Philippi and all round the Ægean Coast. It was, perhaps, natural that he should sail in the same ship with Paul from Troas to Philippi ; but it is soon evident that no chance association bound him to Paul. If he left him, it was not for long, and when he joined him again, some seven years later, it was to share with him shipwreck and imprisonment, and to part with him on earth no more. " Luke, the beloved physician," was doubtless in constant requisition. Paul was always suffering from his eyes—always overworking himself—sometimes prostrated with what we should perhaps call epileptic fits. Indeed, there could be no more suitable companion than a travelling doctor for one whose " outward man was perishing " and " who died daily." His wide acquaintance with men, and the varied experiences of a doctor's life, made Luke peculiarly fit to record the spread of the Gospel (as he does in the Acts) amongst men of different nations. For, Gentile as he was, he was pretty fair to the Jews and in hearty sympathy with the Roman Government, whilst having an intimate acquaintance with the Greeks, especially of Asia Minor. He nowhere mentions himself by name, and seldom even alludes to himself at all. Beneath the modest " we " which occurs in a few chapters of the Acts, the beloved physician is effaced rather than concealed, but the pathos of those few words—dictated by such an one as " Paul, the aged," in prison—" Only Luke is with me," are sufficient to make his name dear and immortal, even if he had not left behind him such a priceless diary as the Acts, and such a prose poem as the Gospel which bears his name.

III.

LUKE, THE PHYSICIAN'S STORY.

ROUGHLY stated for recapitulation, Mark's Gospel was written for Jews and Gentiles, in Greek, between 70 and 80, by Mark, after Peter's death at Rome. Matthew's Gospel was compiled in Greek, from Mark. It embodies *Logia* bearing Matthew's name, derived from oral and written fragments, and issued in Syria, for Jewish Christians between 80—90. I now apply myself more particularly to the date, the sources, and the characteristics of St. Luke's Gospel.

44.
RECAPITU-
LATION.

DATE.

Luke first emerges as the companion of Paul in the Acts. As a medical student he might have known Paul about 52, then in 94 he would only be about 60. We cannot place the date of his Gospel much before or much after 94, for the following reasons :—

45.
ABOUT
A.D. 94 ?

First, he tells us that he wrote only after "many had taken in hand to set forth" Gospels. He had come across many oral and written narratives, amongst them one by St. Mark ; St. Mark he uses copiously and unmistakably ; but St. Mark was not before 74, therefore St. Luke is not before 74.

Secondly, the connection between the fall of Jerusalem and the re-appearance of the Son of Man at the end of the world is maintained, though somewhat modified—the end of the world being a little put off.   Still, after the fall of Jerusalem has been detailed, and the signs of the last judgment closely connected therewith (Luke xxi. 9, 23, 25 ; Luke ix. 27, and compare Matthew and Mark— Mark xiii., Matthew xxiv.), it is plainly recorded that the generation whom Christ addressed should not pass away till *all* (not only the siege of Jerusalem, but also the end of the world) *these things* should be fulfilled; but in 94 most of Christ's contemporaries had passed away — by 100 probably all.   St. Luke's statement could therefore not have been registered with any show of probability much later than 94..

Were Christ's words not fulfilled ? Are they set down in their right connection ? Are they Christ's words at all ? These questions have needlessly perplexed many commentators—a class of persons who are in the habit of making difficulties where none exist, and slurring over or ignoring the real ones.

On the face of it, Christ is made to say that the world should come to an end, that He should re-appear in glory within the lifetime of many of His friends; on the face of it, no such thing took place (*see* sermon on " Hell " in " Speech in Season "). But this question has been merely raised inciden-tally as fixing the date of St. Luke, by showing that a certain statement could not have been made after a certain date. St. Luke is not before 70, is not after 100—is probably about 94.

SOURCES.

Shall we now watch St. Luke at work? Irenæus tells us (A.D. 160) that he wrote out the substance of the Gospel St. Paul was in the habit of preaching. Paul was a learned man, he was well up in literature, sacred and profane; he possessed so rare and fertile a literary gift that we almost wonder he did not himself compile a Gospel. Perhaps he did. Perhaps it was amongst the parchments which he left at Troas, and which came into Luke's hands in those last terrible days

46.

PAUL'S
GOSPEL.

when Demas had forsaken him, and only Luke was with him. We cannot tell, but we know that Paul wrote, dictated, travelled about with MSS., put Gospel fragments into "forms of sound words," of which he has left us more than one exquisite specimen in his Epistles, notably the account of the Last Supper and the appearances of Christ after death.

Perhaps Paul actually succeeded in recovering those parchments ("especially the parchments") along with his cloak. If this was the case, we may be sure that so elegant a scribe as Luke would keep his eye on them, and take care that Paul did not leave them behind him again. Poor aged Paul! What time the care of all the churches came upon him daily, he would sorely need some tried and vigilant youthful friend about him to see after his scanty travelling bags and their miscellaneous contents!

47.
PAUL'S
TRAVELLING.

Indeed, his friends seemed anxious not to leave him alone. As he grew old his infirmities increased, and the thorn in the flesh did not depart —his temper too was a little hasty. He got not unnaturally rather bitter with Alexander, the coppersmith. His memory was not good. He could not quite recollect whether he had baptised certain people or not. He sometimes forgot to pack up all his things, even his Χιτών or mantle, the most indispensable garment in a climate where chills and fevers are so frequent and so fatal! Even his MSS., of such priceless value, some of them probably unique. So his friends seldom allowed him to travel alone. Now it was Tychicus who acted courier, now Timothy, but generally some young man, such as John Mark, the evangelist and profitable for the ministry, and last, but not least, Luke, who doubtless as nearly saw the last of him as any of his friends.

In that late touching Epistle to Timothy (which, with Canon Farrar, I cannot but believe genuine), written from Rome just be- 48. fore the second trial, in the presence LUKE AND MARK AND of Nero, which ended, as is generally PAUL'S thought, in Paul's execution, we read, PARCHMENTS " Only Luke is with me," and " Take Mark and bring him with thee." This was about 67, and Peter was still alive, so that Mark had not yet written his Gospel, which was only composed from memory after Peter's death. When Mark arrived Paul was probably no more, but we can well believe that he may have met and conversed with Luke. Together they may have gone through Paul's literary remains in the house of Clement (still to be entered from the Crypt of S. Clemente at Rome)—together they may have copied and laid by some of his Epistles. At that time Mark may have secured that fragment on the Last Supper out of 1 Corinthians xi. 23-25, which was woven subsequently into his Gospel.

At any rate, we can well imagine that from this time the relations of Mark, the first of the synoptists, and Luke, the last, remained uninter-rupted, and it is certain that Mark's Gospel, when it appeared, soon fell into Luke's hands, and he has, in fact, incorporated almost the whole of it in his own compilation (except vi. 45; viii. 26, and the Passion.)

Amongst the " eye-witnesses " to whom Luke alludes as giving him his accurate information 49. "from the first " were no doubt LUKE'S "EYE- Mark and, perhaps, Peter, who may WITNESSES." have come to Rome with Mark—for Mark stood in the same relation as travelling companion to Peter aś did Luke to Paul.

With such companions we need not add that Luke would gain ready access to those stores of oral and written tradition which he had long been accumulating, to be worked up at last in such a masterly style thirty years later.

Did Luke, writing at Rome (90—100), make any use of the Gospel of Matthew issued in Syria (80 — 90) ? Probably not. Mark's   50. Gospel (70 — 80) got more readily LUKE USES MARK, NOT from Rome to Syria, to be used MATTHEW. by Matthew (80—90), than Matthew, compiled in Syria (80—90), was likely to get from Syria to Rome and be used by Luke (90—100). As in these days the Provinces care far more for what goes on in London than London cares for what goes on in the Provinces, so in those days Syria was likely to get what was written at Rome much sooner than Rome was likely to hear of what literature was being circulated in Syria. If Luke, in 94, had not amongst his " many " versions of Christ's sayings and doings the particular compilation bearing Matthew's name, a compilation more fit for Jews than for Luke's Gentile readers, we need not be surprised. In fact, as we read Luke we perceive that he incorporates the whole of Mark (with one or two omissions before alluded to), and that he adds nothing from Matthew which is not really to be found in Mark; what reads here and there like a fragment of Matthew is either an amplification of Mark's text or so modified as to bear the impress of a different source. Luke stands in the same relation to Mark as does Matthew, but he stands in no relation at all to Matthew—had he seen Matthew he would have hardly broken up the connected utterances of our Lord into fragments, and attached those fragments to times, places, and situations other than are described by Matthew. Luke was reading, and selecting, and arranging for himself out of a mass of oral and written tradition, a good deal of which was neither in the hands of Mark nor Matthew; for about one-third of Luke is new material, to be found in neither of the other synoptics.

The sources of Luke (90—100, at Rome) are (1) Paul's words and memoranda. As Irenæus

51.
SUMMARY
OF LUKE'S
SUCCESS.

says, A.D. 180, "Luke, the follower of Paul, preserved in a book the Gospel he preached " — (2) Mark's Gospel —(3) various ragments and accounts which many others had undertaken to write, amongst them possibly (4) an early Hebrew Gospel, now lost, and (5) such oral tradition as Luke might have gathered from Peter and other eye-witnesses.

CHARACTERISTICS.

Luke's work is more than a compilation—it is a literary work of art. The best form is selected. His version of parable and proverb is the survival of the fittest; no more perfect words could be found than those chosen for the parable of the Prodigal Son, the episode of Martha and Mary, the story of the man who went down from Jerusalem to Jericho and fell amongst thieves. We can fancy the delight of the catechumens in committing to memory such complete and idyllic fragments—they are made for the memory and they nestle close to the heart! Luke requires before all things a rounded whole—a coherent narrative—and he aims at something like a consecutive biography. Speeches are evidently attached to events, more because they seem to fit them than because they really belong to them; here and there a little amplification helps the sense or rounds off the situation. Episodes are

52.
LUKE'S
LITERARY
METHOD.

not only worked up to, but are set-off, cut, and polished like gems, with many facets, surrounded by skilful chasing. Those touching bursts of Hebrew song are inserted to grace and herald in the arrival of the world's Saviour. "The Nunc dimittis" of old Simeon, the "Benedicite" and "Magnificat" of the holy women, are specimens of a literature peculiar to the Jews, of which the Psalms of David remain for ever the glory and incomparable models. The speeches placed in the mouths of different persons by Livy or Cæsar are examples of a similar method, but without the homiletic unction which made the Hebrew haggadistic literature, as Emanuel Deutsch says (Talmud article, *Quarterly Review*), "a comfort and a blessing."

The influence of Rome and the Roman atmosphere is very apparent throughout Luke. He 53. loves order, he even approves of the RESPECT FOR ROMAN hierarchy. The spectacle of the dis-AUTHORITY. cipline of the Roman army and police inspired him, as it inspired his contemporary, Clement, then, or soon afterwards, Bishop of Rome, with admiration. His narrative is so coloured as to bring out the bright side of Roman

official and military life. The Centurions are
open to good impressions; there is no necessary
bar between the army and the church. The
Roman Governors, even Pilate, are fairly dealt
with, and, by a skilful turn, Luke avoids saying
that the Romans crucified Jesus. "The chief
priests and our rulers," says Luke, "delivered
Him to be condemned to death, and have crucified
Him"—that is his last word upon the subject.
Luke's instinct was correct, it was the reflection
of Paul's. He too saw clearly that the future of
the church lay with the Gentile. The torch of
religion had already been handed on from Jerusalem to Rome. Every barrier between the
Gentile world and Christ — Jewish ceremony,
bitter shock of nationalities, synodical disputes,
awkward collisions between Christian interests
and Roman authority—must be toned down, and
Luke is careful to do this.

Luke is an ardent partizan of Paul, perhaps a
little at the expense of Peter. The two great
Apostles began already to stand out as
rivals; they headed two schools of
Christianity, the Petrine and Judaic,
the liberal Pauline or Gentile; but Peter's

54.
ZEALOUS FOR
PAUL'S
HONOUR.

G

authority was at first considered the greatest, and Peter's Christianity by far the most ortho-dox. This is the point silently but effectively combatted throughout Luke's narrative in the interests of his great master, Paul. It was the fashion to run down Paul in Judeo-Christian circles. Some said he was no Apostle at all. Had he seen Christ, or been taught by Him? Had he ever worked cordially with the Apostles at Jerusa-lem? Had he ever been chosen one of the twelve? The answer could hardly be doubtful. The two great Apostles may have never urged their differences to an open breach, but Paul spoke in no measured terms of the Apostles at Jerusalem, "*who seemed to be pillars, but added nothing unto him*"; and on one occasion, we know, withstood Peter to the face because he was to be blamed—whilst Peter looked a little askance upon brother Paul and his Epistles, "*in which were some things hard to be understood*"; and which never were understood at Jerusalem.

Luke feels that Paul's Apostolate must be saved at all costs. He remembered how hard Paul fought for his own dignity in the 2 Corinthians xi. 22, "Are they Hebrews? so am I,"

&c. Paul was as good as Peter. No doubt Peter is to be ranked first in the list of the twelve, but the famous σὺ εἶ Πέτρος (Thou art Peter), &c., need not be constantly harped upon, and it is judiciously omitted by Luke altogether.

Well, but the gifts of the twelve Apostles were unique, and Paul was not one of the twelve? That did not matter. Matthew and Mark may represent them as unique, but Luke shows that the very same gifts were given to the seventy—Commission to preach, to work miracles, to cast out devils ; and what was given to seventy might surely be given to such an one as Paul, and *was*, moreover, given by special revelation. But did Paul work miracles? Nothing very definite or remarkable is recorded, but Luke is careful to mention in the Acts that certain of Paul's doings did pass for miracles; besides, no great stress could be laid upon this, for when the seventy came back elated by the miracles they wrought, had not the Lord Himself said " Rejoice not that the spirits are subject unto you, but rather rejoice that your names are written in Heaven." The most precious gifts, after all, were the spiritual gifts, which none could deny to Paul. Those were the true signs of his Apostolate.

G 2

In Luke we first begin to breathe freely. His
is a universal message for the outside world. His
is the Broad-Church Gospel quite as

56.

PARTIALITY much as the Ephesians is the Broad-
TO GENTILES. Church Epistle. The religion of Christ
is, after all, shown to be a divinely natural
religion. It is the love of God and the love of
man; a love not conditioned by chances of time
or place, but universal, good for the Gentile as
well as for the Jew; nay more, specially good
for the Gentile, because he appeared more ready
to absorb and to distribute it.

The time of the Pharisees was over, a good
time was at hand for the Gentiles—sinners, outcasts, aliens, every one who had been trampled
upon for years was now going to be converted
and live. The narrative is instinctively selected
and arranged, so as to produce this large and
liberal reading of the Gospel. In Matthew and
Mark the Samaritans are looked on as enemies, the
preachers are told not to go into their villages, but
to appeal to orthodox Jews only; but in Luke it is
the good Samaritan who looks after the wounded
man, and the orthodox Priest and Levite who
pass him by.

In Luke the Publican and the Pharisee both go

up into the Temple to pray, but the Publican alone goes down to his house justified.

The woman who was a sinner is forgiven, seeing that she washed the Lord's feet with her tears and wiped them with the hairs of her head.

Zacchæus, the Publican, is accepted because of his earnestness. In Luke and Matthew both thieves blaspheme on the cross, but Luke records how one was, after all, converted; and he points out that Christ prayed even for His murderers: "Father, forgive them, they know not what they do."

It is the Gospel of a universal embrace—of pardon and peace and reconciliation for all—the lost piece of money is found, the lost sheep is rescued and brought home with rejoicings, the prodigal son returns to his father's house, and there is joy in the presence of the angels of God over one sinner that repenteth! And as he (the Gentile) that had abased himself is exalted, so he (the Jew) who had exalted himself is abased. The parables point this moral: The chosen people had said "We will not have this man to rule over us" —well, the King would come and miserably

57.
A PACIFIC
GOSPEL.

destroy them. They thought that because Messiah had taught in their streets and ate and drank with them, they would rank first in the new kingdom. Not at all; others were more worthy. Men would come from the north and south and east and west, and sit down with Abraham and Isaac and Jacob in the kingdom, and the children of the kingdom would be cast out where there was weeping and gnashing of teeth; and, as Luke wrote, that gnashing of teeth had already begun—Jerusalem was a ruin—the Temple was gone—the Jews were dispersed; for centuries their fragmentary history is with difficulty collected, as they lie scattered amongst the nations. The piteous record is stained with blood and tears, and bitter persecution which has broken out afresh in this nineteenth century with new weeping and gnashing of teeth. So, with Luke, the transition period we noticed in Matthew has already passed. In the atmosphere, and at the time in which he writes (though not in the events which he relates), the Temple is a dust-heap—Christianity has passed from Jew to Gentile, the religious sceptre from Jerusalem to Rome—that is to say, from a narrow sect to a religion claiming the allegiance of all mankind. Christ Himself ceases to be merely the Jewish Avatar, He has become the King of all men and the Saviour of the world.

This gigantic transformation has been in reality effected by Paul. The law with its ceremonies, the Jew with his prestige, are with him things of the past. To all Mosaic law, philosophy, and religion, Greek or Roman, there is but one crown and close, one conquering rival—"Jesus Christ, and Him crucified." He is all in all ; He dwells in the heart ; His riches are unsearchable.

What did it all mean ? What *does* it all mean ? It meant that in that age the accidentals of Christianity must fall off; and in that age its alliance with Judaism did fall off for ever beneath Paul's touch. It means that in this age the accidentals of Christianity must fall off, much of the peculiar dogmatic clothing suitable to another world of thought, which Paul gave it, must fall off ; Christianity changes, but after each transformation Christ re-appears. His spirit is essential; His Gospel eternal. Christ, not Paul, is, after all, the eternal Founder of Christianity. Christ, not Paul, corresponds to an eternal necessity of the soul. He alone is the same yesterday, to-day, and for ever.

58.
THE ETERNAL
AND THE
TRANSITORY.

What is that necessity which changes not, even as He changes not ? It is the belief in a God of love; it is a conviction that He has revealed Himself through human nature; it is the belief in a God-communion; in a conviction that He may be found; that belief is ever on the wane, and is ever more and more indispensable; all religions which lose it die, and those which claim it not become degraded or cease to be religions at all. The love of God was latent and lost in Judaism ; Christ restored it to its position, and gave it a human significance it never had before. It had entirely died out of the mythology of Greece and Rome. In those narrow temples (look at the temple of Vesta at Rome, for instance) we can easily see there was no room for the people; they had nothing to do with, nothing to say to the gods, and the gods had nothing to say to them—the world's heart was grown cold and heaven silent. Christ filled both. He made men feel that in the immense unknown something there was which cared for man and palpitated for him. He so spake, He so *was*, that men were able to believe that God was their Father. And nothing short of this will do; we need some One unto whom we may give the whole allegiance and passion of the soul — Who will draw it out, feed it, satisfy it. Christ declared there was that in God which could do this. He professed Himself as so filled with this incarnate side of God's love to usward as to stand in our presence as the God-man—the chosen and divine instrument of exhibiting to man what God was, what God meant—as far as it was possible for us to lay hold effectively of Him and to conceive of His human side at all.

From this new and vivid conception of God's sympathetic humanity flowed the new command to "love one another," which is the keynote of St. John's Gospel and Epistles, and the cornerstone of the Christian edifice.

The new idea is firmly seized in the third Gospel, though not elaborated. We have parted company with the old world; here is no longer any trace of a divided conscience; he taketh away the old that he may establish the new—the transition is already accomplished in the Gospel according to St. Luke.

IV.

JOHN,
THE FISHERMAN'S STORY.

JOHN, THE FISHERMAN'S STORY.

No.

'John, the Fisherman.
59. St. John's escape.
60. St. John at Ephesus.
61. Men who had seen John.
62. Tradition about St. John's Gospel.
63. A Foreigner's mistakes.
64. More Foreign peculiarities.
65. Conclusion about St. John's Gospel.
66. Mr. Matthew Arnold quoted.

CHARACTERISTICS.
67. Meaning of Gnosticism.

No.
68. Gnostic Influence.
69. The Æons.
70. The λόγος.
71. The Paraclete.
72. Memories and Commentaries.

THE STORY OF THE SHEPHERD AND THE SHEEP.

73. The Good Shepherd Parable.
74. The Door Parable.
75. Fidelity and Incoherence.

JOHN, THE FISHERMAN.

PROBABLY the least educated of the Evangelists, he had
not, in the most receptive period of his life, Mark's knowledge of town life, or Matthew's acquaintance with busi-
ness, or Luke's professional skill and wide sympathy with
men. He was a Galilean, an ardent soul capable of close
devotion. He was one of the three always to be found
near Jesus. He had singular opportunities of observing
Him—with Him in the death chamber of Jairus' daughter,
at the grave of Lazarus, on the mount of transfiguration,
by the stones of the Temple when their doom was pro-
nounced. He lay on His bosom at the last supper; he saw
the last agony in Gethsemane; he heard the last cry from
the Cross; the quick instinct of love told him first whose
was the dim form on the shores of the lake seen through
the morning mist a few days after the Crucifixion. He
took the mother of Jesus to his own home. He lived to
pass through the Neronian persecution, which proved
fatal to Peter and Paul. From the rocky Isle of Patmos
he wrote in veiled language' (for fear of the Romans) the
story of Rome's crimes and the church's struggles, beheld
through the lurid fires of persecution and crimsoned with
the very blood of the Saints. He lived long enough to see
the temporary decline of Pauline Christianity at Ephesus
and throughout Asia, and some think, not without reason,
that he shared that fear and distrust of Paul and his
liberal Christianity, in common with the Judaic Christians,

who seemed to go about undoing Paul's work wherever
they could.   Paul seems to have had little or no personal
relations with St. John at Jerusalem, and not much to
do with the others, indeed he had a poor opinion of their
judgment, and none at all of their theology.   With John's
temporary ascendancy at Ephesus and throughout the
churches of Asia, Paul's influence suffered a check from
which it did not recover until the essential sterility of the
Judaic Christianity became apparent, towards the end of the
second century, along with non-fulfilment of the prophecies
in the Apocalypse.   Meanwhile St. John has left in that
same Apocalypse, one of the earliest of the New Testament
writings, a priceless key to the feelings and expectations of
Jewish Christians A.D. 68, whilst in the Gospel which bears
his name, put into elegant Greek at Ephesus by some
accomplished scribe, we doubtless have the most precious
memories of A.D. 30-33, though carried through half-a-
century of oral tradition, and set at last in a written
account which, in its homiletic form, appealed widely to the
Gentile world of the period, although it came out as the
manifesto of Conservative Ephesians.   Still, St. John's
Gospel really joins hands, through its mystic philosophy
and spiritualistic tendencies, with Paul, the great Apostolic
agitator, who overthrew the Jewish barriers and claimed
the Divine mission of Jesus for the world.

IV.

JOHN, THE FISHERMAN'S STORY.

WHEN the fires of the Neronian persecution of 64 paled, everything Christian in Rome seemed to be paralysed or banished. The Christians who could get away fled to the coast of Ephesus, and settled down in the little Jewrys sprinkled throughout Asia Minor. Seven of these we are familiar with through the Epistles to the Seven Churches.

Tradition relates how St. John, after narrowly escaping martyrdom at Rome, reached Ephesus, and spent the remainder of his life between that city and the Isle of Patmos, revered as the centre of the Asian Church and the last of the twelve Apostles.

With the nightmare of Rome still upon him—his imagination filled with the visions of blood and fire he had so lately witnessed—in the full stream of all the startling rumours that came

60. from the city of Rome in ruins in the ST. JOHN AT west, and the holy city of Jerusalem EPHESUS. besieged by the Roman armies in the east—the Apostle thundered forth that tremendous invective known as the " Book of the Revelation," in which, to the eye of the discerning historian, the events, or rather rumours of events, then transpiring in the east and west, week by week, are so faithfully and even minutely mirrored. The curious, rough Hebraic Greek of the Apocalypse—so unlike the polished Ephesian or Athenian Greek of the Johannine writings—is probably the nearest approach we shall ever make to the dialect in which the old fisherman of Palestine tried to convey his ideas to the rising generation of Ephesians.

What a strange new centre was that city of Ephesus for the Apostle John now growing old—

61. John, the last depository of such price-MEN WHO less memories, an object of irresistible HAD SEEN JOHN. attraction and reverence to men in intellectual culture far his superiors. It is easy to picture him to ourselves, surrounded by eager young Greeks, well versed in the forms of academic or the metaphors of Gnostic philosophy to which the Palestine Jew was a total stranger. How would his talk about our Lord be likely to come out when translated into their scholastic dialect, or represented and illustrated by the current conceptions and watchwords of the Gnostic philosophy or philosophies? Presently we shall see.

With the dawning years of the second century—Jerusalem still a heap of ruins—Rome very nearly rebuilt—the fruitful seed of Christianity sown throughout every Jewry in the Empire, what time the raging dispute between the followers of Paul and Cephas and John was at its height, the aged Apostle himself passed away. No one was now left who could say, " I have seen HIM."

But through the luminous mist which hangs over the events 100—120, certain dim figures arrest our attention—men whose boast it was to have known the Apostle, like Polycarp; to have retained much of his talk, like John Presbyter and Aristion, who seem to have learned quantities of John's' sayings by heart. So Polycarp, 160, was never tired of declaring, " This I hold from the Apostles," and " I who have been taught by the

H

Apostles, and have lived with many who knew Christ," &c.

Are we now nearing the written rills—the oral freshets of the fourth Gospel? We are. That **62.** celebrated fragment known as the **TRADITION ABOUT** Canon of Muratori describes Luke **ST. JOHN'S** and *John's* Gospels, and if we place **GOSPEL.** its date as late as 175 we may still be pretty certain that it bears witness substantially to what men like Papias, Polycarp, Aristion, and John the Presbyter were in the habit of saying between 100 and 160. This, then, is the earliest tradition (175) concerning a Gospel of St. John: " The fourth of the Gospels is by the disciple John. He was being pressed by his fellow disciples and (fellow) bishops, and he said: 'Fast with me this day and for three days, and whatsoever shall have been revealed to each one of us let us relate it to the rest.' And in the same night it was revealed to the Apostle Andrew that John should write the whole in his own name, and that all the rest should revise it "*—which amounts to this, John wrote last, under some pressure, and his friends

---

* Muratori fragment—authenticity denied by author of " Supernatural Religion," accepted by Mr. Matthew Arnold.

revised his work. The tradition of A.D. 175 hangs well together. John probably talked more than he wrote; perhaps he could not write at all; perhaps the Apocalypse itself is dictated; but if so it remains probably a very literal transcript of the Apostle's Greek patois—whereas the Gospel (or many parts of it) remains a very much revised transcript of the Apostle's memoirs.

The tradition, I say, hangs together, but the Gospel, as we have it, hardly bears out the tradition, if we take the tradition to imply that John superintended, approved, or ever could have had read out to him the Gospel which now bears his name. There are certain things in that Gospel as it now stands which John, the fisherman, who witnessed the crucifixion, never could have passed. Put the case.

Aristion reads: "These things were done in Bethany (early MSS.), beyond Jordan . . ."

"Nay, brother Aristion," saith the aged Apostle— who might have listened with a radiant smile to the glowing eloquence in which the Greek scribe had embodied the mystic relations between the "Word," the "True Light," and the eternal

63.

A FOREIGNER'S MISTAKES.

H 2

"Father"—"Nay, brother Aristion, we will accept thy strange and glorious speech concerning the blessed Master—who was indeed the life, the light of men, and the word of God—but *Bethany* is not beyond Jordan, 'tis but fifteen stadia from Jerusalem, and we have often walked there with Lazarus in the cool of the day."

The error was so obvious (just the error which a Greek might make about a village in Palestine) that the later MSS. of John have *Bethabara*, which is beyond Jordan ; but the three earliest MSS. have "*Bethany*," which is no doubt the original reading.

The phrase "a sponge on hyssop" is another case in point—hyssop was a close flowering bush like a sponge. The writer had heard of hyssop and the blood of sprinkling, but did not exactly know what hyssop was, so makes it do duty for the "cane" of the synoptics, on which a sponge was raised to the dying Saviour's lips, and virtually says "they put a sponge upon a sponge ! " St. John, who had seen crucifixions, would never have let that pass.

Suppose Aristion again reads :—" To Caiaphas, who was the High Priest that same year. . ." " Nay, but 'tis not a yearly office," the Apostle

would surely have pointed out, and the stylus of
Aristion would have been at once drawn through
the words "*that same year.*"

Yet it was as natural for a Greek at Ephesus to
suppose that the High Priest's was a yearly office
like a consul's, as it might be for an Englishman
not very well up in American politics to fancy
that the President of the United States of
America is annually elected.

Again, Aristion reads: "That disciple (*i.e.,* a
friend of Peter, the fisherman) was *an acquaintance of the High Priest,* and went in with Jesus to
the palace of the High Priest."

"Stay! The High Priest—the proud Sadducee
—O brother Aristion, could have no such friends
as the lowly Peter and his associates; nor could
such even come near enough to gain his ear, or
enter his palace, save as menials and slaves."
In fact, such a confusion of ranks as is implied
by a fisherman being on easy terms with the
High Priest must have sounded as incongruously
in John's ears as would the following in ours:
"Now there was a certain man selling newspapers outside Buckingham Palace during the
levée, and that man happened to know a
baker's boy who was a friend of the Lord

Chamberlain, and so they both went in to the Palace together."

These are the kind of mistakes which foreigners make when they write about English matters, especially matters of social rank, which they imperfectly understand. Do we not read in the French newspapers how "*Lord Bright* made a great speech against primogeniture," and "sir Gladstone was most eloquent about things in general?"

Again, we can hardly imagine St. John himself always speaking of his countrymen, the Jews, and

64.

MORE

FOREIGN

PECULIARITIES

their customs, not as would a Jew, but exactly as would a foreigner— a Greek or Roman. We read how the waterpots of Cana "were set after the manner of the purifying *of the Jews*," as a Frenchman might observe—"the manner of *English* policemen is not to wear cocked hats and swords, but helmets and wooden truncheons." Or, "There arose a question between some of John's disciples *and a Jew about purifying*," as a German might write—"I was present at a discussion between Mr. Gladstone and *an Englishman* on the Khartoum affair about Gordon." "They wound the body of Jesus in linen clothes, with spices, as *the manner of the Jews is* to bury," as an Italian might observe—"The *English* don't bury as we do, with torch processions by night, but in broad daylight, and the body is borne to its last rest in a long black box on wheels, called a 'hearse,' and the *English* are particularly partial to ostrich feathers dyed black, and attendants of doubtful sobriety carrying long black canes, with scarfs, silk hat bands, and gloves!"

A Jew would no more speak of the *Jews'* Passover than an Englishman would allude to the "*Englishman's* Tower of London," or the Englishman's Derby day.

We are, then, it seems, bound to conclude that John's Gospel, in *its present form*, could not have been written by John, or even read aloud to him after it had been written; but the tradition itself extant about it, and the character of the Gospel, at once enable us to claim it as substantially St. John's material; and that this is so will appear, and in what sense it is so will appear. St. John's Gospel is genuinely St. John's, in spite of the manifest Greek editing; says Muratori's

65.
CONCLUSION
ABOUT
ST. JOHN'S
GOSPEL.

fragment (*cir.* A.D. 175), "that John should write
and the rest should *revise.*"   Nowhere as in the
Apocalypse do we read, "John to the Seven
Churches," or "I, John"; but always it is a second-
hand statement on the face of it, and generally the
third person is used, thus—"He who hath seen
hath borne witness, and *that man* (the Greek
editor, Aristion or John Presbyter, perchance)
knoweth that he saith true, that ye may believe."
The Presbytery at Ephesus, who issued this
Gospel, say about 120 A.D., speak here :—"This
is the disciple who testified these things, and
who wrote these things, and we (who now issue
the disciple's compilation in the form of this
Gospel of St. John), we (the Elders of Ephesus)
know that his testimony is true."

To the simple Bible reader, with the most
superficial knowledge of the circumstances, the
66. matter, the authorship, approximate
MR. date, test of authenticity and im-
MATTHEW
ARNOLD portance of this Gospel must, I
QUOTED. think, now be apparent.   In the clear
words of Mr. Matthew Arnold, whose argument I
have followed above :—"The Gospel is John's,
because the whole value is in the *Logia,* the say-

ings of the Lord, which it saves, and by John these *Logia* are furnished; but the redaction — the present form—is not John's, and could not be; and at the beginning of the second century, when the work appeared, many there would be who knew well that John's the redaction was not. The redaction, with its unity of tone, its thoroughness and connectedness, is by one single hand— the hand of a man of literary talent, a Greek Christian, whom the church of Ephesus found proper for such a task; a man of soul, also a theologian, perhaps a theological lecturer."

That neither John nor any of the Gospels are certainly quoted in their present form before the second half of the second century proves, as Mr. Matthew Arnold points out, rather that they were still undergoing revision than that they did not exist. Indeed, the church must have been engaged in a series of constant Gospel revisions and emendations, and naturally so, as long as ever there was on the earth any one who had conversed with those who had seen Christ. All such had probably passed away before A.D. 200, and before that time, say by 180, the date of Irenæus, the slow but complete disengagement of the planetary Gospels of Matthew, Mark, Luke, and John from the confused nebulæ of miscellaneous writings had taken place, representing the last survival of what the Christian conscience decided to be the fittest.

CHARACTERISTICS.

But the chief fascination of John's Gospel must always lie in his peculiar presentation of God in

**67.
MEANING OF GNOSTICISM.**

Christ. The new Christian theology is here expressed in the manner of the time—the thoughts and words of the aged Apostle are translated for him by the philosophers at Ephesus into the current phraseology of the schools. Gnosticism was just then the rage. No theory of religion could possibly escape its influence—it aspired to embrace and formulate all theories of religion—it has left its deep and, I may say, sublime traces upon the Gospel of St. John. And what was Gnosticism? We should call it a kind of Eclecticism. It was the result of Greek, Egyptian, and Asiatic religions combining with Judaism and at last taken up into Christianity.

Anything wilder and vaguer than Gnosticism at first sight can hardly be imagined—yet is it full of harmonious thoughts, and one clear thread of passionate intention runs throughout the tangled web. What is that thread? It is the ceaseless longing—perhaps one of the most "deep-seated in our mystic frame"—to connect the Ineffable God with His own Universe and with Man.

"O that I knew where I might find Him." "How unsearchable are His judgments, and His ways past finding out." "Show us the Father and it sufficeth us." "The invisible things of Him from the foundation of the world are clearly seen, being understood by the things which are made—even His eternal power and Godhead." And "God was in Christ, reconciling the world unto Himself." "He sent forth His son, born of a woman, born under the law." How to conceive of God—how to connect Him with this world—how to explain His dealings with man—how to read His self-manifestations—how to draw nigh unto Him?

All the dreams of Gnosticism, which when duly catalogued and put into English appear absurd, laboured, or repulsive, become softened down and even pathetic when viewed as the passionate struggles of the finite spirit—moving about in worlds not realised, and aspiring with the most insatiable longing to know God.

I will take a few of the strong lines in the complex Gnostic system, or rather systems ; and it will

68.

GNOSTIC

INFLUENCE. then be easily seen how skilfully they were used to emphasize certain aspects of Christianity, and create for it a metaphysical basis of which it stood just then in sore need.

First, then, to the Gnostic, there was the ineffable God, dwelling in the light, unapproachable. Out of the Pleroma or fulness of that light proceeded Æon after Æon—these were vaguely impersonated attributes of Deity—giving birth to ministers of a more directly personal character, such as the Demiurgos, who was identified with the *Jehovah, or God of the Jews*, a being responsible for this world and all it contains. *Here Judaism was fitted into the Gnostic system.*

This world and man were not the immediate creation of the Ineffable One, but of this inferior Demiurge, who contrived our world — a very mixed and imperfect affair, full of pain and contradiction. Matter seemed to be the chief stumbling-block, and the Ineffable One in His great goodness sought to remedy the work of the Demiurge, and so sent one of His great divine Æons, by name Christos, or the anointed one, who, descending upon the man Jesus, sought through His ministry to save the whole race by bestowing upon them a spiritual life which should lift them above the bondage and supremacy of matter. This was the victory which overcame the world, even their Faith. Faith was a loving trust, and hence spiritual union with the conquering *Æon Christos* — revealed in Jesus—and *here Christianity was fitted into the Gnostic system.*

The doctrine of the Paraclete or divine emanation, "the Comforter," went very well with the doctrine of the Christos Æon resting for awhile on Jesus—for when Jesus had passed away, the Christos Æon could re-appear in the form of the Paraclete or Comforter, " If I go not away the Comforter will not come, but if I go away I will send Him unto you." The chief Gnostic heresy, or the " *A mare aliquid,*" lay in the Gnostic denying to Jesus anything but a phantom existence, and thus depriving us of our real consolation in the conviction that He was tempted in all points like as we are. This phantom view is by *no means endorsed in John's Gospel*, but the Gnostic influence is sufficiently apparent in the opening verses of the Gospel, " In the beginning was the Word," &c. We cannot be too thankful for such language, its expressions stand for something very real, substantial, precious, and altogether indisputable and true. Indeed, a kind of joy as of discovery comes over the religious teacher when he is able to point out in the musings and meditations of the past what, in such ancient attempts to express religious truths, remains constant, the same "yesterday, to-day, and for ever."

Gnosticism has given to Christianity a meta-physical framework—*i.e.*, in other words, the neces-sary and indispensable law of its thought-order; it has united this to an historical manifestation in Jesus of Nazareth; it has indissolubly connected His mission with an inward and spiritual realiza-tion in the doctrine of the Holy Ghost, the Comforter, a doctrine corresponding to the deepest needs, experiences, and aspirations of the soul.

I will now briefly emphasize the great Gnostic outlines, as in the hands of a cunning draughtsman

69.
THE ÆONS.

they are made to resume the main features of Christian theology in the opening of St. John's Gospel.

First, there is the σοφία, Wisdom, or λόγος, the

Word—to the Gnostic a *created Æon* (=heresy), to the Christian an *ever essential* (= orthodoxy) portion of Deity. That is the *first* difference between the systems. This Word in St. John is an inherent attribute of the Ineffable One, dwelling with Him in the heaven, the unapproachable Light. Now the Divine Wisdom or *Word* stands for the expression of moral and spiritual qualities intelligible to mankind—*justice, love, knowledge, goodness*—qualities to which we all attach definite meaning, though our definitions of them may somewhat vary. Here, then, Gnosticism outlines for us in its own striking but faulty manner the first and most precious Christian doctrine, which is *the essential and eternal existence of intelligible human attributes in the Ineffable One.* His Being might mean far more; it might involve creation and interest in other worlds, but it meant, at all events, interest in Humanity. *" In the beginning was the Word, and the Word was with God, and the Word was God.*

Secondly, the coming forth of the *Logos.* Such sign of the Ineffable as could be realised under human limitation in due time comes forth—the *Christos* rests on the *Jesus.* But the Jesus is not to us a phantom, as He was to the Gnostic.

Hence the *second* point of distinction between Gnosticism and Christianity. To remedy the confusion, to take away the sin, to save man from the evil influences inherent in matter, the Ineffable interposes—but our Christos Æon is combined with a real man. "The Word was made flesh, and dwelt amongst us, and we beheld His glory, the glory as of the *only begotten* of the Father (hence *third* difference between Gnosticism and Christianity, since according to the Gnostic there were *many begotten*), full of grace and truth."

The assertion is further developed in the words of Jesus—betraying the profound personal consciousness of His being as the divinely accredited exposition of the human side of God—a witness to the truth that God had a human side, and could therefore approach man and be received by him. This never leaves Jesus as He comes before us in St. John. The brief and Gnomic " The Word was made flesh " is developed by the Master, thus—" I came forth from God and am come into the world," &c. The certainty that in the divine and human mind σοφία, wisdom, λόγος, divine utterance and manifestation—in other words, that goodness, truth, justice, mercy—meant the same thing in heaven as on earth, that there was a common language, a common sympathy between God, the Creator, and man, the created, is further emphasized in the words, "I and My Father are one"; "He that hath seen Me hath seen the Father." The absolute moral unity of divine and human ideas is here forever proclaimed and impersonated.

Other leaders and guides of men have given us partial illustrations in a lower sphere of the method adopted by Jesus in manifesting forth on earth the human nature of God. I remember hearing and seeing Garibaldi, in the midst of a revolutionary crowd, point to himself with at once the most personal and impersonal action of his life, and say, " I am liberty." In the same way a judge on the Bench might say, "In me you behold the Majesty of the Law—I am Justice!" And so in St. John the third and last Christian doctrine is emphasized, the doctrine of *communion between the Creature and the Creator*, the open passage between God and man was proclaimed by the revelation of the Human Nature of God. He who came revealing it said, and said truly, "I am the Way, the Truth, and the Life"; "I am the Door." Through such a door—

the open door of God's Humanity—we can
alone enter in. "No man cometh unto the
Father but by Me." That is literally true. God
must be conceived of as eternally human—and
manifesting Himself as such—the common ground
must be so reached before ever we can come to
Him. Thus even before Christ—before, as the
Gnostic would have said, the Christos Æon
descended on Jesus—the human side was plainly
revealed; it was ever through that alone that
the world of men had held converse with God,
in so far as they ever had done so. This is
the eternal fitness of Christianity. It is not a
question of whether we *will* or *will not* have a
human God; you *must* have a human God, for
you cannot transcend the limits of your own
mind, and nothing save what is human and derived
from human conceptions can your mind entertain.
The only question is whether you will conceive of
a bad human, or half-bad, half-good, or a wholly
good human God—between such three conceptions
(always human) man has frequently wavered. The
ideal which has won is that which declares God
wholly good in *our* sense of the word—wholly
loving, wholly wise. History has received an
indirect and vague, but none the less deep and

indelible, impression of this divinely human side of the Ineffable. History identifies that impression with Jesus of Nazareth, the King of the Jews. St. John's Gospel gives Him to humanity in these words—"In Him was life, and the life was the Light of men."

There was yet a *fourth* Christian doctrine, appropriated and emphasized by the Gnostics. It was the doctrine of the Paraclete or Spiritual Presence — God immanent. When John's Gospel appeared, the generation who thought they had the promise of Christ's re-appearance in final judgment had passed away. More true to history, more true to spiritual life, was the doctrine that the Christos Æon would come again to His disciples as the unseen Comforter, the hidden well of water springing up unto eternal life. The outward manifestation was then over. In John we find no dream of a remote future advent. The spirit was come at last who should abide with them for ever, and help them to carry on that victorious struggle with matter which they had seen accomplished in the person of the Divine Teacher, when He said—"In the world

71.
THE
PARACLETE.

I 2

ye shall have tribulation, but be of good cheer,
I have overcome the world."

The Apostle had indeed tarried till He came.
He had lived to see the sign of the Son of
Man flash from Jerusalem to Rome,
coming out of the east and shining
even unto the west. And he was
quite ready for his *Nunc dimittis*. Pre-
cisely what he dictated before his departure,
about the beginning of the second century, we can
never know. How much was written down at the
time, how much afterwards from memory, we can
but infer ; but by the time the mass of Johannine
memoirs came up before the Ephesian Syndicate
for final revision and issue, towards the middle of
the second century, and the Gospel of St. John
emerged in its present form—we can safely say that,
although the voice may be that of John, the fisherman, the hand is the hand of an elegant Ephesian
Scribe, a Greek theologian, "a man of soul" with
a tendency to teach and explain. We can here and
there lay our finger on the point where he flies off
into exposition on his own account, as in Chapter
iii. 16, where the *aside* runs : "*For* God so loved
the world," &c. ; and it is very difficult to read

72.

MEMORIES
AND COM-
MENTARIES.

through such chapters as the xvii. without feeling that the hand of the amplifier and expositor for edification has been again at work. But whatever has been thus done has been well done. The Greek theologian had a thorough taste for such homiletic writings. With the Gnomic sayings of Jesus, the parables, the Hebrew haggadistic method of Jesus, the Greek Scribe had less sympathy. We shall find him more than once at fault.

As a compiler he is beneath Mark, and as a combiner far below Luke. It only requires a fresh eye and a knowledge of the Synoptic reports to re-arrange approximately some of the material which has got mixed together in John. Mr. Matthew Arnold has attempted this, I think, with considerable success, in the parable of the Good Shepherd (John x. 1).

The Story of the Shepherd and the Sheep.—John x. 1, &c.

Here are evidently two groups of sayings, one starting from the image "I am the *Good Shepherd*"; the other from "I am the *Door.*" 73.
In each group there was a shepherd, THE GOOD SHEPHERD a door, and sheep; but in the Door PARABLE. parable there was a "*shepherd*" and "*the*

door" and "*the sheep,*" and in the Shepherd
parable there was "a *shepherd, a doorkeeper, a
door,* and the *sheep.*" These two groups are
evidently distinct and have as evidently got mixed
up; they are distinct, because in one there is a
door by which the shepherd goes in, in the other
there is a door through which all must go in who
would be saved. In the *Door* parable Christ is
the door and the religious teacher who follows
Him is the shepherd. In the *Shepherd* parable
Christ is the Shepherd of the sheep who enters
into the fold by the door of the heart—"Behold I
stand at the door and knock."

So these two groups are distinct; but, secondly,
it is clear that they are here mixed and hence the
confusion of the passage as it stands in our Gospel,
for there Christ is made to be at once the door and
the shepherd; He may be both, but not both in
the same parable. If He is the door, then in that
parable He cannot be the shepherd that goes in
at the door; if He is the shepherd then in that
parable He cannot be the door at which the
shepherd goes in. To re-arrange these sayings
we must place the verses thus :—*The Shepherd
parable,* ½-11, 3, 4, 5, 8, 10, 11. *Door parable,*
7, 1, 2, ½-9.

Preface the Shepherd parable with some such fragment as ½-11 ("The Good Shepherd giveth His life for the sheep"), then read on "To Him the porter openeth and the sheep hear His voice and He calleth His own sheep by name and leadeth them out, and when He putteth forth His own sheep He goeth before them and the sheep follow Him, for they know His voice, and a stranger will they not follow, for they know not the voice of strangers. All that ever came before Me were thieves and robbers (Sadducees and Priests, *see* St. James), but the sheep did not hear them. The thief cometh not but for to steal and to kill and to destroy. I am come that they might have life, and that they might have it more abundantly, I am the Good Shepherd," &c.

Begin at verse 7, which is evidently a repetition of the "Verily, verily" of verse 1, thus : "Then said Jesus unto them again, verily, verily, I say unto you, I am the Door of the sheep. (1) He that entereth not by the door into the sheepfold, but climbeth up some other way, the same is a thief and a robber; but he that entereth in by the door (*i.e.*, the true *teacher* and *follower* of Christ) is the

74.
THE DOOR
PARABLE.

shepherd of the sheep. (9) I am the Door, by
Me if any man enter in *he is the shepherd of the sheep.*"
Not, as in the text "He shall be saved and shall
go in and out and find pasture"; this belongs evidently to those who are led by the Good Shepherd,
Christ—not to those true shepherds who follow
Christ in leading the sheep to pasture who are
saved, being themselves the pastors of the flock.
Verse 9 and verse 2 are evidently identical in
structure—combine the two, and you get this :—
(verse 9) "I am the Door, by Me if any enter"
(verse 2) "*he is the Shepherd of the sheep.*"

The Greek Scribe lacked the familiarity with
Christ's ways that we seem to catch from reading

75.
FIDELITY
AND
INCOHERENCE

the Synoptics—*e.g.*, John xiv. 31 :
"Arise, let us go hence," and then
we get three more chapters of
discourse; "*arise*" was evidently a common
phrase of Christ's. "Rise, let us be going"
occurs in Matthew. The "arise" is undoubtedly
genuine, but here in John xiv. 31 it is wrongly
placed, for no one goes. This literalness and
fidelity to some fragment, *at the expense* of coherence,
is found elsewhere in this Gospel.

In John iv. 43, where Jesus is said to go into

Galilee, "*for*" He testified that a prophet had no honour in his own country; that *for* is misplaced, it ought to be, and He *went* "*notwithstanding*" that He testified that a prophet had no honour, &c.; yet the "for" could hardly have crept in here in defiance of sense had there not been some saying properly clinched with "for He said that a prophet," &c.

The use of the word οὕτως, "thus," is also very suggestive of literal fragments. Jesus sat "thus," as I have been telling you, by the well. John leaning "thus," as I have been telling you, on His breast. But there has been no such telling, nevertheless these were undoubtedly the traditional words of John, and they are retained, although their exact connection has been lost. For the foregoing criticisms I am indebted to Mr. Matthew Arnold's "God and the Bible."

Lastly, in this coronal Gospel we seem to stand looking up into heaven. It is the Gospel of Transfiguration. In it the Word made flesh has already passed into spirit and into life—but only that He may return as Comforter, to remain with us for ever. This is the Christ of the Gospel according to St. John.

V.

LUKE,
THE PHYSICIAN'S DIARY.

LUKE, THE PHYSICIAN'S DIARY.

No.

SCOPE AND COMPASS.
76. " We " of the Diary.
77. The human ever in God.
78. The Panorama of the Acts.

AUTHOR AND DATE.
79. Publication why delayed.
80. Publication why resolved upon.
81. The Acts in Embryo.

No.
82. Reticences of Luke.

CHARACTERISTICS.
83. Luke's Democratic feeling.
84. Luke a Reconciler.
85. Good men agreed in heart not head.
86. The simplicity which is in Jesus.
87. " Christianity " and " Christ.'

V.

LUKE, THE PHYSICIAN'S DIARY.

SCOPE AND COMPASS.

THOSE chapters of the Acts marked by the use of "we," the graphic and personal monosyllable indicative of Luke's presence as an eye-witness, stamp the Acts with the value and interest of a diary. The instant the reader thus comes upon the traces of the beloved physician he is made to feel that he is face to face with one who has "a perfect understanding of all things from the very first." Acts takes up the closing notes of the Gospels and repeats them. The events described range from A.D. 33 to about A.D. 63-4, but the record detailing them is probably as late as 90, and it was written most likely at Rome, far away in time and place from the scenes and many of the personages described.

Two theological positions stand as sentinels at the entrance to the Acts. The first is that Christ

Jesus lives in God, that the human side of God

77. which was before the man Jesus was
THE HUMAN
EV^E R IN
GOD. not extinguished by the death of Jesus
—death had no power over that—the
grave could not hold it. It always *was*—it was
manifested on the arena of earth—it always *is*, this
human side or aspect of the Deity—and it remains
the same yesterday, to-day, and for ever.

Secondly, a real "processional" work of the
Spirit followed the removal of Jesus. Through
this Spirit the human side is still with us—or as
the Gnostic theologian would have put it (here-
tically no doubt), the Æon or Divine emanation
which settled upon Jesus re-appeared in the person of the Holy Spirit descending in tongues of
fire upon the followers of Jesus, "all of them
being filled with the Holy Ghost."

The vision of the early church, as it appeared
to contemporary eyes, is then made to pass before

78.
THE
PANORAMA
OF THE ACTS. us in a series of graphic pictures. The
peace and content of the little circle—
its early communistic organization—
the first trials and collisions with the outside
world—the martyrdom of Stephen. Then, after
the panic and momentary dispersal of the

Jerusalem group, comes the spread northwards to Antioch—Antioch, first "Christian" city, with its seaport town of Seleucia and its mixed population—Antioch full of all the vices, but also forming a ready *nidus* for the incubation of all sorts of new ideas. Such towns have always been the great sites of propaganda—Corinth, Ephesus, Alexandria, Rome, Antioch, and next to the unsophisticated provincial towns of Greek origin in Asia Minor, such as Lystra, Derbe, and Iconium, Christianity has found in seaports and capitals like these its heartiest welcome.

Presently we shall see the Gospel winging its way across the Mediterranean—Saul sailing to Cyprus; but the Acts of the Apostles will then have become merged in the Acts of the great Apostle to the Gentiles. Into Paul's career I shall not here enter, as I devote a future volume to him ["The Picture of Paul"]. His historical life ends with the Acts, about A.D. 64, at Rome, where "Paul dwelt two whole years in his own hired house and received all that came to him."

AUTHOR AND DATE.

I have placed Luke's Gospel A.D. 90-4. Now Acts, according to its own preface, was issued *after* the Gospel; but both Acts and Gospel were

79.   probably coming together in the note-
PUBLICATION   books of the beloved physician ever
WHY
DELAYED.   since the death of Paul (*cir.* 68), and
in all likelihood some time before.   Parts—how
much it is impossible to say—may have been
in writing for several years, and even handed
about, copied, and re-copied, in some sort common
property, but only issued when the importance
of such records began slowly to dawn on the
Disciples, owing doubtless to the delayed coming
of Christ, and the deaths of so many who had
known Him.

If it did not seem worth while to write down
the words and deeds of the Master, much less
important must have appeared the Acts of his
followers.

Paul disappears about 68.   Luke had been his
friend (and latterly his constant companion) for

80.   about sixteen years.   Luke may, in
PUBLICATION   A.D. 68, have been about 43, and had
WHY
RESOLVED   in his possession, about A.D. 70-5, all
UPON.   needful records for both Gospel and
Acts — but he delays publication.   There were
already, he tells us, quantities of records floating

about. Many were alive who remembered Jesus, and others flocked to hear details from their lips (so Papias tells us); written documents were far less exciting and popular, they existed in private circles, but the outside demand for them was not yet very great. How often (it cannot be too frequently repeated) are people the depositories of memories, the importance of which neither they nor their friends understand. How comparatively seldom even now, when so much is printed, are they invited to write their recollections down. But by A.D. 94 it may have occurred to Luke that too many of the Lord's friends had dropped.

After the fire of Rome, after the flight of the Christians to Pella, after the siege of Jerusalem, after the death of Paul (and Christ not come yet!), Luke may well have thought the time was ripe for authentic written records such as Matthew's "words" and Mark's "deeds." And Luke himself was growing old; and so, as we conjecture, in A.D. 90, when the Evangelist and doctor may have been about 67, he issues his Gospel, following that up in about A.D. 94 with his Acts.

81.

THE ACTS IN
EMBRYO.

K

The Acts may have been coming together or collected in fragments really before the Gospel, although it was published after it.   The fact is, our Bible order of arrangement is confusing, with its Revelation at the end of the text, and its Acts after John's Gospel, and Matthew before Mark. We suffer from a cheat of chronological perspective; we must never forget in reading the New Testament that the *events* dealt with are one thing, and the *time of their written relation* quite another. But my reader will, at any rate, have learned this much—if he has in the least grasped my aim and method—that a knowledge of the *mise en scène*, the author, and the time of writing is, in the case of the Gospels, Acts, and Epistles, only second in importance to the subject-matter itself.

In the two following volumes, entitled " The Picture of Jesus " and " The Picture of Paul," I have never lost sight of this cardinal position, and it entirely affects the colouring, as it is bound to do, and sometimes even the actual drawing of both those pictures.

As regards the late date now assigned to the Acts, A.D. 94, it may firstly be asked—Why have we no allusion to Paul's death in Luke's Diary ?

The answer is, probably—*from prudential reasons.*
Paul's death, *cir.* 68, was doubtless
the great crowning scandal, from the
Christian standpoint, of Nero's last
year—known to everyone in Rome; for that
very reason all allusion to it would be carefully suppressed in Domitian's reign, when Luke
published his Acts.

We note a similar reticence in Clement's Epistle
about all the persecutions of Domitian. Although
he was in the thick of them, his Epistle makes
hardly any allusion to what was going on; he,
like Luke, was always most respectful to the
authorities; but Luke would have had to condemn
the Roman Governors the instant he spoke of
Paul's martyrdom, so he said nothing. John's
Cryptograph is the most striking proof of the
mingled terror and respect which the Christians
had for Roman authority. In the Revelation the
sternest sentence is passed on Nero; but his very
name is so carefully concealed in cypher, and the
language is so allegorical and veiled, that without an historical key the Apocalypse is quite
unintelligible—and even with a key, and the
right key too, the meaning is not always very
clear.

K 2

CHARACTERISTICS.

In Acts we are far from Judæa. The geography of the Holy Land is loosely understood, the

83.
LUKE'S DEMOCRATIC FEELING.

Rabbinical lore is doubtful. Luke did not know much of the one, and he cared nothing for the other. The same democratic feeling which stamps his Gospel betrays itself in the Acts. The popular theory is kept well to the fore. The *people* (*sic*) would have received Christ, it was the rulers and the priests who stood in the way.

Everywhere there is a wide sympathy with the Gentiles. The future of the church is felt to lie with them. Luke's respect for the Roman officials and the Roman government is quite Pauline. Gallio, the Corinthian magistrate, the Ephesian town clerk, the Roman soldiers, the Roman Governors, even Felix and Aggrippa appear to advantage. The Roman police and officers are kind to Paul, the judges are indulgent and conciliatory. One hears him gladly, another wishes to set him at liberty, a third only wants a little bribe, but means no harm to Paul.

Luke is a great pacificator. He ignores as much as possible the discords between the Jewish and nascent Pauline factions. The account of the Jerusalem council, presided over by James, is probably the most roseate view of what really took place. There the Gentiles are supposed to be finally let off circumcision and treated as brethren, Paul having represented that it would not do to saddle them with such Jewish rites. Paul, man of the world—travelled man—emancipated from national prejudices, seeing the future, eager and prescient— according to Luke, got very considerable con- cessions for the Gentiles out of James and the Apostles, at Jerusalem, in open council.

84.
LUKE A
RECONCILER.

But we are able to check Luke's account, in Acts, with Paul's own account of the same council, in Galatians. If Gentiles were so liberally to be dealt with, and it was so decreed in open council, what is the root of bitterness which rises at Antioch ? Why does Peter cower before the emissaries of James and dissimulate, first eating, and then refusing to eat with the uncircumcised ? If Luke's account is *quite* correct, Peter, when he ate with the uncircumcised, was merely doing just what the Jewish council, with James for mouth- piece, had decided should be done—letting off the Gentiles. But no sooner do Paul and Barnabas (and, for a moment, Peter) assume that the Gentiles are to be let off than down come emissaries from Jerusalem, insisting on circumcision, and all the rest of it.

What is the meaning of Paul's circumcision of Timothy, a Greek ? Why, here Paul makes a clear concession to James's party, which would have been quite needless had James really given up circumcision in open council. But the fact is, the circumcision question never was settled at Jerusalem or anywhere else. The Jewish faction *always* stood out for Jewish rites, and was for forcing them upon the rising church of the Gentiles. Paul *always* opposed them, although for peace and quiet he made one concession after another ; but the real differences between the Jewish Apostles and the great missioner to the Gentiles were fundamental and irreconcilable. Still, some show of personal peace and friendship seems to have been kept up during the lifetime of Peter and Paul—chiefly, no doubt, through the efforts of such men as Barnabas and Luke and Silas, and perhaps John Mark ; and this composing, conciliatory instinct was a true one.

Luke had that spiritual perception (which is

even now too rarely found) that the good men who
differed were really deeply agreed,   85.
in faith and feeling, in conduct and   GOOD MEN
                         AGREED IN
devotion; that Christianity was, after   HEART NOT
all, a moral more than a doctrinal   HEAD.
reform — a Life before a Creed — and that all
things must be done for edification rather than
for the triumph of this or that party in the
church, the will of God being not so much our
Orthodoxy as our Sanctification. Place at his
disposal the facts, and a few years of perspective,
and a true spiritual interpreter like Luke will
make all the pious disputants say very much the
same thing. Paul will agree with Peter (in spite
of his own Epistle to the contrary, Galatians),
and James will side with Paul, and settle everything amicably; although subsequent events may
tell too plainly that nothing ever was settled, and
that all that took place at the Jerusalem Synod,
with the best intentions on both sides, began and
ended with " words, words, words ! "

Although, practically, the " Acts " are the
Acts of Paul only, and all "Acts" attributed
to the rest are not " Jacobite " or " Petrine " or
" Johannine " at all, but " Pauline," yet with the
surest insight and spiritual tact, Luke's chronicle

of events passes as the "Acts of the Apostles."
Dignified and fitting at length is the outcome of
those Acts according to the statement of our
"beloved Physician," for the Acts strike the
essential key-notes of a world-wide religion,
laying no great stress upon its vanishing Jewish
form, its local and fugitive controversies, its
infertile Judæan branch.

In Acts the purpose and story of a great moral
reform stands out clearly. Its pages are full of
calls to repentance, full of gracious and wide
invitations " to you and to your children, and to
all that are afar off, as many as the Lord our
God shall call "; full of edifying episodes and
fragments of admirable discourse and affectionate
exhortation. " Repent ye and be converted, that
your sins may be blotted out " (iii. 19). As Luke's
is the Broad-Church Gospel and Paul's Ephesians
the Broad-Church Epistle, so is emphatically Acts
the Broad-Church commentary. " Of a truth," it
says, " God is no respecter of persons " (x. 34);
and the Christian Religion seems, for a moment,
almost independent of doctrine, and identical with
high-toned sympathetic morality, when it can be
said that " Pure religion and undefiled before God
and the Father is this ; to visit the fatherless and

the widow in their affliction, and to keep himself unspotted from the world!"

How sweet the light that steals across the darkness of the ages from those early days! How clear and crystalline well up still the fountains of living waters from those distant hills! As I turn the sacred pages I can see once more the love of God in the face of Jesus Christ. I find there, beneath the incubus of nineteen centuries of theological subtlety and rancour, at last the simplicity which is in Jesus; and I can build once more my Church of Christ " upon the foundation of Apostles and Prophets, Jesus Christ Himself being the chief corner stone."

86. THE SIMPLICITY WHICH IS IN JESUS.

Sometimes theologians tell us—" If you want to discover what *Christianity* really is you must go back to the age of Constantine, to the fourth century, to the proper formulation of the Faith, to the Nicene Creed." I reply, " yes—no doubt; but if you want to discover what the *religion of Christ* is, you must go back to the age of Tiberius and Nero, to the first century, to the New Testament, to the words of Jesus, and to the Acts of His Apostles."

87. "CHRISTIANITY" AND "CHRIST."

VI.

JOHN, THE FISHERMAN'S CRYPTOGRAPH.

JOHN, THE FISHERMAN'S CRYPTOGRAPH.

No.

THE AGE OF THE APOCALYPSE.

88. Before the Vision.
89. Special value.
90. Revelation not before A.D 68.
91. Revelation not after A.D. 70.
92. John the Apostle is the writer.
93. Why the "Fathers" object to this theory.
94. Revelation no forgery.
95. John a "Son of Thunder."
96. Peculiarities of style and language.
97. Summary.

THE SEVEN CHURCHES.

98. Little Apocalypses.
99. Their tendency to recur.
100. The revelation built on Daniel.
101. The "Angels" of the Churches.
102. The Seven Epistles—a Jewish and Anti-Pauline Manifesto.
103. Paul's death made a difference.
104. Jewish Christianity.
105. The inevitable severance.
106. Strained relations.
107. Paul in self-defence.
108. A bitter application.
109. Paul on Meats and Marriages.
110. Paul on Circumcision.
111. The breach delayed.
112. The fire breaks out.
113. The survival of the Fittest.
114. Paul and "the Reformation"
115. Two cardinal but mistaken beliefs.

No.

THE GREAT DRAMA.

116. The Beasts and the Elders.
117. The strong Angel.
118. The Book and the Lamb.
119. An historic retrospect.
120. The Red Horse.
121. The Black Horse.
122. The Pale Horse.
123. The cry of the Martyrs.
124. Silence in Heaven.
125. The Seventh Seal.
126. The first trumpet.
127. The false Nero.
128. The Parthians.
129. The Temple measured off.
130. The close again postponed.
131. The Seven-headed beast.
132. The Great Cryptograph of Nero.
133. Thrust in thy Sickle.
134. The Seven Vials.
135. The Scarlet Woman and the Beast.
136. Imperial and Pontifical Rome.
137. Rome is judged.
138. Satan is bound.
139. Gog and Magog.
140. The Kingdom come at last.
141. The Crystal River and the Tree of Life.
142. The Spirit and the Bride.
143. The one Clear Note.
144. Letter and Spirit.
145. Immediate impression.
146. Why Revelation lost ground.
147. How Revelation regained its place.

VI.

JOHN, THE FISHERMAN'S CRYPTOGRAPH.

THE AGE OF THE APOCALYPSE.

BEFORE giving an account of the Apocalypse or Revelation of St. John, I shall clear the way by fixing the date and authorship, and shall describe the peculiar atmosphere in the heart of the Roman Empire, out of which the vision arose, together with the meaning of its introductory Epistles to the Seven Churches of Asia. This will bring us to the opening of the celestial drama at the beginning of chapter iv. Rev.

88.
BEFORE THE VISION.

First, I notice that the Apocalypse is the earliest of the Evangelistic books (A.D. 69), for though it stands at the end of the New Testament, it is earlier than any of the Gospels (earliest Gospel being by St. Mark, A.D. 75). The Apocalypse was

89.
SPECIAL VALUE.

preceded doubtless by the Apostolical Letters, and followed by the four Gospels, but as a record of early *Church* feeling and opinion, it is superior to the Gospels, and equal to the Pauline Epistles (A.D. 52—67).

The Revelation was probably written by, or immediately under the direction of, the Apostle St. John, at Patmos, where he seems to have lived some time in exile. It was published to the world at Ephesus, early in the year 69 A.D. That I believe to be a brief but fair statement of the latest results of modern criticism.

90. REVELATION NOT BEFORE A.D. 68.

First as to the date. We can fix it almost to a month. It could not have been before 68, or after 70 A.D.

How do we know this? It could not have been before 68, because it alludes to events which took place in 68, and early in 69.

Nero committed suicide, A.D. 68.

Nero is the seventh head of the beast in chapter xiii., and the Seer writes, "I saw one of his heads as it were wounded to death." His death was widely disbelieved in throughout the Greek Islands, and a false Nero arising (68 and 69 A.D.), the report that Nero was alive quickly spread, so we read (Rev. xiii. 3) " His deadly wound was healed : and all the world wondered after the beast." As I shall show when I come to that part, the accession of Galba, the stampede from Jerusalem, and other events of 68, together with the struggle for the Empire in the Spring of 69 A.D., all go to fix the date not earlier than these events—not earlier than the Spring of 69.

Much later than 69 it could not be, for, as I shall by-and-bye show, the writer seems unaware of Otho, who succeeded Galba 15th January, 69, and writes as if the return of Nero—after the fall of Galba on the 10th January—was an accomplished fact ; a fact, however, which never took place, as the real Nero died in June, 68, and the false Nero met with his death about 16th January, 69.

All this will be clear enough when we come to deal with the portions of Revelation referring to these events.

Revelation could not have been written after 70 A.D., for it describes the permanence of the temple and the triumph of the chosen of Israel, and in 70 A.D. the temple was destroyed and the Jews irrevocably scattered.

91.
REVELATION
NOT AFTER
A.D. 70.

We stumble here upon the very key of the Apocalypse. It was a profound conviction that, after the death of Nero, the Roman Empire would collapse, the Jewish Christians would triumph gloriously, and that, although in the struggle the enemy might tread down their city and even the outer gates of the temple, yet that God's Holy Temple itself would never be taken or destroyed (Rev. xi. 1, 2). The Book of the Revelation recording the ultimate triumph of the Jewish Christians, and the collapse of the Roman Empire, could not have been written later than 70 A.D., and, in fact, after the disastrous events of 70, resulting in the dispersion of the Jews, and the re-settlement of the Roman Empire, the Book of the Revelation was suppressed probably by its author, because it was seen to foreshadow a number of events which were therein predicted as immediately to follow (Rev. xxii. 10; i. 1), and which did not follow, and could never follow. And so the Apocalypse was suppressed for many years, and only revived with the revival of persecution, after which, as I shall by-and-bye relate, its position was very ambiguous, until Joachim de Flore in the eleventh century gave it a new lease of life, by inventing for it the still popular view, which supposes it to be a description of events still in the future, a fantastic opinion, which will no doubt soon receive, if it has not already received, its *quietus*.

Fixing the date of publication in the Spring of 69 A.D., we next ask—what reason is there to suppose that the Apostle John was the author?

(Revelation i. 9), "I John, who also am your brother, and companion ¦in tribulation, and in the kingdom and patience of Jesus Christ." Who is this John? Either he is the Apostle, or he is a person assuming the Apostle's name and authority; or he is John Mark, or John the Presbyter. Take the last two suppositions first. John Mark never had enough to do with the churches of Asia to adopt the authoritative tone of Revelation to the Seven Churches. In spite of Ewald's high authority, we hold with M. Renan that the shadowy figure of John the Presbyter, which haunts the Church of Ephesus, to the confusion of the critics, is not the John of the Apocalypse. An obscure passage by Papias, and an apologetic thesis by Denys of Alexandria, are hardly enough to build upon. Such a man, speaking with such *aplomb*, would have found a place in the Gospels, in the Acts, would have been heard of at Jerusalem. One whose knowledge of Jerusalem, of Rome, of Ephesus, whose position in each is so well defined, is certainly a chief leader, an Apostle of the first class, no mere John the Presbyter. That some such editor or amanuensis, escaping from Jerusalem in 68 A.D., might have found a refuge at Ephesus, and had a hand in the Gospel or Epistles attributed to St. John, is possible; but the same hand is distinctly not in the Gospel and in the Apocalypse, for the Apocalypse is the most Jewish and the Gospel the most Greek of all the New Testament writings. The theology of the first is most Petrine, that of the other most Pauline, and, between these two, as we shall see, is a great gulf fixed.

The Greek fathers of the third century were glad enough to attribute the Apocalypse to John

93.
WHY THE
" FATHERS "
OBJECT TO
THIS THEORY.

Presbyter, because they could not bear its intensely Jewish and anti-Greek and Roman tone. Such opinions of the Gentile world as are expressed in the Apocalypse it was needful at all costs to deprive of Apostolical authority; but such considerations have no weight now. We reject, then, as authors of the Apocalypse, John Mark and John Presbyter.

Secondly, are we dealing with a forgery? Such forgeries we know to have been common, and not to have been thought immoral in those days. Prophetical writings were thus often ante-dated—*e.g.*, the Apocalypse of Daniel, Baruch, Enoch, Esdras, or the Apocalypse of Peter. In the second century numerous Apocalyptical works were ascribed to the Apostolic age. If the Revelation is in this sense a forgery, it was written either during St. John's life or very shortly after it. It could not have been addressed by a forger to the churches in Asia in the lifetime of John, for such a presumptuous forgery, using the " I John," would have been instantly exposed. Or if we deny with some that John ever presided over the Seven Churches of Asia, still less would a writing in those days affirming this have had a chance. It could not have been written after John's death, because of the first three chapters, which represent the author of it alive; besides, published as it was in 69 A.D., when, had John been dead, it would

94.
REVELATION
NO FORGERY.

L 2

have been known at Ephesus, the forgery would have been too impudent.

Assume that John was dead in 69, and the writer of the Apocalypse makes him describe events which took place after his death, how would people who knew he was dead treat that? What credit should we give to a letter criticising Marshal MacMahon's ministry and bearing the name of Napoleon III.? Why, none at all, for we should say the writer forgot that the Emperor died before the events he is made to comment upon occurred.

The forgery theory then, which in the case of other early writings is usually plausible, is, in this case, almost impossible, for it is hard to see how it could have been issued in the Apostle's lifetime by another, and harder to see how it could have been issued after his death in his name.

One fact, at least, stands out in spite of some adverse criticism—that John the Apostle had very close relations with the churches of Asia. For if he wrote the Apoca- lypse this is certain, and, if he wrote it not, it is equally certain, since it would have been senseless, in the year 69, to

95.

O N
"Json of
THUNDER."

attribute to John, in addressing the churches, a position which everyone knew he had never held. The Apocalypse is quite as personal to John as the Corinthian Epistles are to Paul. Truly, it is the voice of the son of thunder, full of fiery vengeance. As in his Master's lifetime he had wished to call down fire from Heaven to consume the Samaritans (Luke ix. 54), so now in his vision he beholds fire mingled with blood fall upon the earth (Rev. viii. 7), and a lake of fire (Rev. xix. 20) receives the enemies of Jesus Christ. He who forbade men to cast out devils, unless they followed the immediate little Christian band with him (Mark ix. 38), was also the most unfavourable to teachers like Paul, " which say they are Apostles, and are not" (Rev. ii. 2), simply because Paul and his followers followed not with him, as others in Christ's lifetime had followed not with him. He calls them no true Jews, no Apostles, and leaves him out altogether in speaking of the Apostles of the Lamb (Rev. xxi. 14).

He who aspired to sit on a throne with Christ in His Kingdom (Mark x. 37) is still the same, whose wholly unaltered view of heaven consists of the paraphernalia of an earthly court (Rev. xx. 4) —" I saw thrones, and they sat upon them."

He who as a Jew dreamed of nothing but the glories of Jerusalem, is the same who identifies the triumph of Christ with the " New Jerusalem, coming down from God, prepared as a bride adorned for her husband" (Rev. xxi. 2).

He whose hatred of the outer world has been alluded to, and who even in the new heavens and the new earth keeps up the distinction between Jew and Gentile—giving the fruit of the tree of life to the Jew, and only a decoction of its leaves to the Gentiles (Rev. xxii. 2)—is the same who foretold the overthrow of the great Gentile city of Rome—" Babylon the great is fallen, is fallen."

The writer's familiarity with both Rome and Jerusalem is evident enough, and the Greek of the

96. PECULIARITIES OF STYLE AND LANGUAGE.

Apocalypse is just what we should expect from a native of Palestine writing in Greece. It is *thought* in Hebrew and *written* in Greek; it is by one who knew the Prophets by heart, but knew them in Hebrew.

This style was acceptable to Jews, and to Jews only, and may have been partly the work of John, and partly that of an amanuensis under his direction. To reconcile the extreme violence of

the Apocalypse with the proverbial lovingness of
St. John, we have only to remember that as his
love burned brightly for Christ, and those whom
he considered Christ's friends, so did his wrath
burn fiercely against the enemies of Christ and
His church. What looks like qualities mutually
destructive, is, after all, only the same quality
manifesting itself under different circumstances.
Love for one thing usually means hate for its
opposite.

Then, be it remembered, the common view that
John was the Disciple whom Jesus loved, who lay
on His breast, to whom He committed His mother,
is after all only an assumption, though a probable
one, and his character for love and gentleness is
derived entirely from the Gospel bearing his
name, and the Epistles which, whatever memories
they may contain of him, are certainly not by his
hand, as we shall see, although the anxiety of the
Greek Fathers to claim the purer Greek and
more philosophical works as the Apostle's, and to
reject the narrower Judaising Apocalypse, is intelligible enough. One thing, at all events, they
could not fail to see, that the same mind could
not have produced both; but what they could not
or did not choose to see was, that of the two, the

unpopular Apocalypse was incomparably more like the work of the Apostle than the idiomatic and philosophical Gospel; and we decide this for the very reason which made them decide otherwise—viz., the Jewish tone and patois of the one and the Greek tone and idiom of the other.

Putting tradition, fact, and inference together, we may very fairly assume that St. John,

97. SUMMARY. after narrowly escaping martyrdom at Rome in 66, fled to Ephesus, and in the year 68, still filled with the bloody visions of the Neronian persecution, wrote the Apocalypse in a kind of literary cypher, or veiled allegory, in the Isle of Patmos, and sent it through the churches of Asia, just after the fall of Galba, Nero's successor, in the Spring of 69 A.D.

THE SEVEN CHURCHES.

I NOW consider the Epistles to the Seven Churches of Asia, introduced in the usual prophetical

98. LITTLE APOCALYPSES fashion by chapter i. And we shall do well to remember that the Apocalypse is only one fragment of a kind of literature which was plentiful amongst the

Jews and early Christians. Ezekiel had set the model, importing into his utterances, in addition to symbols and symbolical acts, strange visions, abstract and complicated conceptions, connected with monstrous beasts, which remind one forcibly of the Assyrian art and philosophy from which they sprang. Zechariah and Daniel followed, and the popularity and convenience of the new style as an open secret for those with a key, but a closed book to others, fixed the form of all future Apocalypses, such as the Book of Enoch, the Assumption of Moses, &c. Every critical point in Jewish history was met by an Apocalypse, and the same simple idea runs through them all—the coming of the Messiah, the dispersion of His enemies, the triumph of the Saints.

The persecution of Antiochus, the Roman occupation, the rule of the Herods; each in turn roused the Apocalyptic instincts in the Jews, and left its mark on Esdras and the Maccabees. The reign of Nero in the same way registers itself. The "Revelation," Epistles, and Gospels are full of little Apocalyptical fragments, such as 1 Thess. iv. 15, and Matthew xxiv., dating from 50 to 100 A.D.

99.
THEIR TENDENCY TO RECUR.

Later, during the persecutions of Domitian Hadrian, Septimius Severus, and Decius, and even during the Gothic invasions, similar writings will arise.

The form of the Book of the Revelation is therefore not peculiar, but altogether common,

100.
THE
REVELATION
BUILT ON
DANIEL.

and the wonder of the Apocalypse is not its novelty, but the fact that, whilst borrowing its forms, phrases, and ideas from the prophetical writings of the Old Testament, it is, nevertheless, a work of first-class power, and worthy to rank with any of them.

After declaring that the events about to be related must shortly come to pass, the prophet gives us, almost in the words of Daniel (vii. 13), the familiar vision of the Son of Man coming in the clouds, and the margin of our Bible shows at a glance to what extent the Son of Man and His surroundings are borrowed from the prophets Ezekiel, Daniel, and Zechariah.

The exhortation which follows is addressed to the Angels of the Seven Churches. Not the Bishops, I think, as some would understand it, but the Angels

or celestial representatives of the churches, after
the belief of the Jew that each nation,   101.
THE
community, family, and individual "ANGELS"
OF THE
had its angel, or celestial guardian.   CHURCHES.

There is one curious point about the Seven
Churches of Asia. The Churches of Colosse and
Hierapolis are not mentioned. The reason why
Colosse is not included is because it had already
been destroyed by an earthquake, and the important
Christian centre of Hierapolis is not mentioned
because the Evangelist Philip settled down there
and was acknowledged as its chief pastor.
St. John, making a clean sweep of Paul's authority,
only mentions the churches over which he presided. Philip probably was dead by this time,
but Hierapolis is still left out, as belonging to a
distinct Episcopate.

I come now to the Seven Epistles. One reproof
evidently runs through them all. The terms of
the thrust of it are a little varied, but   102.
the spirit is the same. What is the THE SEVEN
EPISTLES—
pith of that reproof? It is aimed at A JEWISH
some teaching by which the churches AND ANTI-
PAULINE
have been corrupted. What is that MANIFESTO.
teaching? We shall soon see; it is the teaching,

if not of Paul himself, at all events of those who claimed his authority. At any rate, bitter opposition to an emancipated Gospel runs through all the seven Epistles. This may be new to some, but it is none the less evident. Follow with attention the cumulative evidence for this assertion.

St. John pleads for Jewish Christianity shackled with Jewish rites.

St. Paul, as we know, proclaimed aloud that he was the Apostle of the Gentiles, and that they had nothing to do as Christians with Jewish observances, and might leave them to weak brethren.

St. John was of the Jewish type of Apostle, and looked upon St. Paul as an outsider, not even alluding to him when speaking of the twelve.

St. Paul, in his lifetime, by a kind of divine tact, never broke decisively with Peter, James, or John, the Jerusalem party. But he had founded Gentile churches in Asia, in the very heart of the Jewrys there. He had never got on with these Jews. Between them and the Jewish Christians there was often a good understanding, but between Paul's emancipated Christians and the Jewish Christians there never was; and when Paul was dead, all the Jewish bitterness against his teaching on circumcision, meats offered to idols, &c.,

burst forth, and seems poured like a vial of wrath into the Epistles to the Seven Churches.

Probably the Apostles face to face would never have come to these sad extremities, but Paul was dead, that commanding, beseeching, controlling, and compelling personality could no more be confronted with John, and John at Ephesus found himself, in his old age, surrounded by the triumphant Jewish faction, and so it comes to pass that the language of appeal to the Seven Churches is quite Athanasian in tone—it seems to me, in short, notwithstanding Canon Farrar's ingenious ante-Nicolaitan *Apologia*, very much like the language of the Jewish dogmatist and the theological partizan.

103. PAUL'S DEATH MADE A DIFFERENCE.

We do not naturally think of Christianity as of a reformed branch of the Jewish religion, an improved kind of Judaism; but the Apostles at Jerusalem considered it as such, and that is why it interested them. The Pharisees disapproved of the murder of St. James, Bishop of Jerusalem, and stood in the same relation to the Christians as the Catholic Church might to the Protestant branch, nay,

104. JEWISH CHRISTIANITY

certain of the Pharisees went even further, for we read (in Acts xv. 5), " There rose up certain of the sect of the Pharisees which believed, saying, that it was needful to circumcise them, and to command them to keep the law of Moses." Cardinal Manning, though differing from the Archbishop of Canterbury, would nevertheless disapprove of him being murdered by the Secularists, or even by a fanatical Catholic.

The Jerusalem Christianity was, in fact, tied on to Judaism ; but Paul saw that the time had come

105.
THE
INEVITABLE
SEVERANCE.

for cutting the old hull adrift. His instinct was to get away from Jerusalem, and so he sailed out in the freedom of the spirit into the wide waters of the Gentile world.

Between two such positions a collision was inevitable. It came in little, sometimes big, shocks, all through the lifetime of Paul; but the Epistles to the Seven Churches announce the great and final severance between the Jewish and Gentile Christianity, the bond and the free Christianity, the old world and the new.

Bearing this in mind, let us turn to the second

chapter of Revelation, " Unto the angel of the church of Ephesus write." This was

the church to which Paul, only five years before, had addressed his famous Broad-church Epistle to the Ephesians, in which he brushes away, like a cobweb, the distinction between Jew and Gentile (Ephes. ii. 14).

Imagine the effect of such an Epistle upon a Judaiser like St. John, jealous for the privileges of the sacred people, and wedded to "the law of commandments contained in ordinances," which St. Paul there declares to have been " abolished " (Ephes. ii. 15).

From what follows we can gather distinctly enough the charges rife in the Christian Jewrys of Asia against St. Paul. The first charge against him was that, being not of the twelve, he was no true Apostle, and the same slur was no doubt cast on the Episcopate of his friend Timothy.

To the Ephesians, fresh from the reading of Paul's epistle, St. John accordingly writes: "Thou hast tried them which say they are Apostles, and are not, and hast found them liars." We cannot fail to recollect the indignation with which Paul, wounded to the quick, retorted to a similar charge: " I was not a whit behind the very chiefest Apostles.

Truly the signs of an Apostle were wrought among you in all patience, in signs, in wonders, and mighty deeds." And Paul, in his turn, makes small account of the Apostles at Jerusalem. Fourteen years after he went up to Jerusalem with Barnabas and Titus; there he conferred with the Judaising Apostles, James, Cephas, and John, and he says, "For those who seemed to be somewhat whatsoever they were, it maketh no matter to me, for they who seemed to be somewhat in conference added nothing unto me but contrariwise," &c.

Paul nearly comes to a rupture with Peter about Jewish observance of meats: "I withstood him to the face, because he was to be blamed . . . . I said unto Peter before them all, If thou, being a Jew, livest after the manner of Gentiles, and not as do the Jews, why compellest thou the Gentiles to live as do the Jews?'" (Gal. ii. 14), and in 2 Cor. xi. 13 he is so far carried away in the heat of self-defence as to declare that those Apostles who would force circumcision on the Gentile world are "false Apostles, deceitful workers, transforming themselves into the Apostles of Christ." And he adds ironically, alluding probably to himself having been called Satan, as he seems to be called (Rev. ii. 9, 13, &c.), "And no marvel; for Satan himself is transformed into an angel of light. Therefore it is no great thing if his ministers also be transformed as the ministers of righteousness." Note the double play of thought, amounting almost to confusion. You transform one who is the messenger of God's light into a Satan, whilst you, who are the real Satans or accursers of the brethren, walk about transformed into ministers of righteousness. Those who in your eyes are Satans are righteous, those (*i.e.*, yourselves) who in your eyes are righteous are the ministers of Satan.

2. Cor. xi. 12, contains another double play in allusion to circumcision, where he says, "What I do, that I will do, that I may *cut off* occasion from them which desire occasion." Compare with a similar allusion (Gal. v. 12): "I would they were even *cut off* which trouble you."

We must admit that although his followers are roughly handled in the Apocalypse, Paul did not spare his accusers, even when they happened to be Apostles. But in the second charge, conveying probably a covert sneer at his boasted Roman citizenship,

107.
PAUL
IN SELF-
DEFENCE.

M

which would certainly not endear him to his countrymen, Paul (if the words are accepted as applying to him) is accused of being not even a Jew. "I know," says the Epistle to Smyrna, "the blasphemy of them which say they are Jews, and are not, but are the Synagogue (*sic*) of Satan."

This charge, and it was no new one, never failed to rouse Paul into a kind of patriotic frenzy. "I speak," he says, "as concerning reproaches." "Are they Hebrews? So am I. Are they Israelites? So am I. Are they the seed of Abraham? So am I. Are they ministers of Christ? (I speak as a fool) I am more," &c. (2 Cor. xi. 22).

But all these charges were as nothing to his great offences against the laws of Moses, and the Jewish rites and privileges. With one sweep of the pen Paul and all his followers are branded with the happy epithet of Nicolaus, and the Nicolaitanes, a phrase handing them all over to perdition, as eating meats offered unto idols and allowing mixed marriages (for which a very offensive term is used), two of Paul's greatest heresies. "So hast thou also them that hold the doctrine of

108.
A BITTER
APPLICATION.

the Nicolaitanes, which thing I hate." "Thou hast there them that hold the doctrine of Balaam, who taught Balac to cast a stumbling-block before the children of Israel, to eat things sacrificed unto idols, and to commit fornication " (*sic*) (Rev. ii. 15, 14).

Balaam, translated by *Nicolaus,* signifies "conqueror of the people," so as Balaam caused the Israel of God to sin through the idol feasts and the heathen women, so Paul, by allowing his disciples to eat meat offered to idols, and to contract marriages with the heathen, was a like seducer of the people of Christ; so St. John, writing as chief Ephesian pastor in 59.

Bearing such accusations in mind, which Paul had to encounter all his life, we can understand the somewhat prolix but earnest argument in 1 Cor. viii., written by St. Paul at Ephesus in 57: "As concerning therefore the eating of those things that are offered in sacrifice unto idols, we know that an idol is nothing," &c. "Neither, if we eat, are we the better; neither, if we eat not, are we the worse."

Paul then goes on to say that we must be tender to the weak brethren who thought it

109.
PAUL ON
MEATS AND
MARRIAGES.

M 2

wrong to eat—an exhortation which could hardly have been soothing to the feelings of the Apostles at Jerusalem "who seemed to be pillars," and who held opinions violently opposed to Paul upon this very question, and expressed them roundly enough in Acts.

Paul's opinions on mixed marriages were equally independent and abhorrent to the Judaising party.

1 Cor. vii. 12 : " If any brother hath a wife that believeth not, and she be pleased to dwell with him, let him not put her away. And the woman which hath an husband that believeth not, and if he be pleased to dwell with her, let her not leave him. For the unbelieving husband is sanctified by the wife," &c. All which broad, human - hearted, and wise teaching, struck out boldly by the far-seeing, practical Paul, was an abomination to the narrower Jew; still dreaming of a little Jewish heaven, with its Messiah, and thrones and crowns for the chosen, and space in the outer courts for reclaimed Gentiles, plucked like brands from the burning, and, of course, to be utterly dissociated from their own manners and customs.

And lastly, there was the great controversy

about circumcision. In the early days, when Paul and Barnabas went up to Jeru-

salem, the vexed question of how far Gentile Christians should conform to Jewish rites was openly discussed. Peter was present, and James, and John, but James presided, and gave judgment (Acts xx. 24). The Gentiles were let off circumcision, but upon them was rivetted the command to abstain from meats offered unto idols, and from blood, and from things strangled, and from fornication; and Paul was commissioned to bear this message to the Gentile world. Why then any further disturbance about circumcision? The answer is, I think, simple enough. Paul, whose opinion of the wisdom to be found at Jerusalem was never very high, went far beyond his commission. Under the stress of his powerful presence, and supported apparently by St. Peter, circumcision, according to Luke, was lifted from the Gentiles; but this was a compromise. The *Jewish* Christians were still bound. The rite was still hallowed, nay, it was even doubly acceptable to Jewish Christians, separating them as the elect from the Gentile world. But no sooner is Paul's back turned on the Council than the spirit and the letter of it are vigorously denounced. He proclaims throughout the churches that " In Jesus Christ neither circumcision availeth anything, nor uncircumcision; but faith which worketh by love (Gal. v. 6). " Circumcision is nothing, and uncircumcision is nothing " (1 Cor. vii. 19). They never admitted that at Jerusalem. That the only really circumcised are those who " worship God in the spirit " (Phil. iii. 3), and most of all, that " There is neither Greek nor Jew, circumcision nor uncircumcision, Barbarian, Scythian, bond nor free, but Christ is all in all." This kind of passionate declamation must have been unutterably offensive to the ears of the authorities at Jerusalem, and who could be surprised if they turned at last and declared that no genuine Apostle, and no true Jew, could have uttered them? But it was the genius of Paul to stand alone, to make his own world, and to forget, in his wider aspirations, the narrow theology of which he had had a taste at Jerusalem. They bore wit him up to a certain point, but when, from under-estimating the Apostles' views on circumcision he proceeded to cast the rest of the treaty to th winds, and to proclaim the lawfulness of eating all meats and maintaining mixed marriages, Paul went far to cut *himself* off from the fellowship of those whom he, in moments of exasperation, desired to see *cut off* from his churches, and the final separation was only a matter of time.

Still, that separation came not in Paul's lifetime. The burning zeal, the convincing rhetoric, always told when he was present in person, in spite of his self-depreciation. The overpowering force of the man's character bore down opposition. As soon as he appeared to answer for himself—the "pillars" were struck dumb or echoed his sentiments. Then there was Barnabas, that son of consolation, with sympathies almost equally Jewish and Gentile, with a true peace-making temperament, and he seems to have acted like a sort of buffer between the opposing sides, thus preventing disastrous collisions, and effecting gracious compromises.

III. THE BREACH DELAYED.

But when Barnabas had gone, when James was martyred, Timothy in prison, Peter and Paul dead, and John alone left at Ephesus, surrounded by Judaisers, the smouldering fire burst out, and the note of irreconcilable antipathy to the Pauline teaching

112. THE FIRE BREAKS OUT.

was at length sounded, in those bitter Epistles to the Seven Churches, which stand like iron sentinels upon the very threshold of the Apocalypse to warn off all the disciples of Paul.

But time has been more just to both the great Apostles than they and their partisans ever could

113.
THE
SURVIVAL OF
THE FITTEST.

be to each other. We remember now, not the Disciple who wished to call down fire upon his enemies, and knew not what spirit he was of; but only the Disciple whom Jesus loved. Paul is no longer the arch-heretic, the enemy of the law, the deceiver of the people, the false Apostle, but the man whose eyes were really opened; the man who, in breaking through the exclusive barriers of Judaism, gave Christianity to all tongues and nations; the great Apostle to the Gentiles, through whose ministry and Epistles the king-doms of this world have, in name at least, become the kingdoms of God, and of His Christ.

In a few years the Judaic Christianity, repre-sented by the Apostles at Jerusalem, became almost extinct, as it was at all times infertile. It perished with the temple and the city; it died with its Hebrew rites and its narrow theology. The star of Paul, after suffering a temporary eclipse, arose upon a new world; a new theology was founded; a new pathway of light was opened. It is true that the Christianity of Rome was, in a heirarchical sense, Petrine, and not Pauline, and that the old spirit of Jerusalem has brooded for nineteen centuries over the Papal See. But, although the hands were the hands of Esau, the voice was the voice of Jacob; although the outward form was of Peter and John—for the hierarchy, the Pontifical authority, the Apostolical succession, are all a kind of Jerusalem and its Sanhedrim over again—yet the voice of dogmatic theology, at once the strength and weakness of the Christian church, the voice that cried aloud to the Gentile world was the voice of Paul; and it sounded loudly in the ears of the great church doctors of the third, fourth, and fifth centuries, and it reached the far-off isles of the Gentiles. It was therefore found necessary to elevate Paul to an equality with Peter.

It was Paul, again, who sounded the note of the Reformation—Justification by Faith; Paul who supplied the food upon which the Protestant churches have been living ever since. For centuries the Apocalypse of St. John and the Epistles of the great Nicolaitan have been bound up in one cover, and read side by side with equal reverence and love. It should make us very humble, and very hopeful, to remember that those good and holy men, who worked for Christ in opposite camps, and almost excommunicated each other, as other good and holy men do now, are at last, by the Christian conscience, seen to be at one in the life eternal. May such a lesson not be thrown away.

114.
PAUL AND "THE REFORMATION"

We must now lay aside all thoughts of St Paul, and prepare ourselves for the great drama which the Epistles to the Seven Churches are intended to herald in. I shall attempt no exposition verse by verse; all I mean to do is, to give the key to the whole position, and an example, by a rough, narrative commentary, of the way we ought at this time of day to read and understand the Apocalyptical visions. The key of the whole position is this—

115.
TWO CARDINAL BUT MISTAKEN BELIEFS.

First: A belief common to St. John and the rest of the Jewish Christians, that after the fall and mythic revival of Nero in 68-69, the Roman

Empire would come to an end, and Rome, the great Babylon, would be destroyed.

Secondly: That the Jewish Christians would then receive back their Lord—none other than the promised Messiah of their nation. That He would come, according to Daniel's prophecy, in the clouds of heaven, with all His holy angels, and that, after sundry wars, the final judgment would be set, and that in about one thousand years the whole scheme of human history would be wound up, and the ultimate celestial reign commence.

History has not verified these expectations. At the same time, we cannot understand the Apocalypse unless we bear in mind this twin belief in the immediate fall of Rome and in the immediate return of Christ. These are the things " which must shortly come to pass" (Rev. i.). From this point we must keep our eyes upon the open Bible. We shall then see how closely the Book of Revelation, amidst all the mystery of it, clings to contemporary history; how it can be read and interpreted by what we know through modern research to have been actually going on at Rome, Jerusalem, and Ephesus, in Gaul, Spain, Greece, and Asia Minor.

THE GREAT DRAMA.

At Chapter iv. the great drama opens. The churches have been aroused, and the Divine vision is now made to pass before them. A door is opened in Heaven. The Seer goes up, he hears the voice as of a trumpet talking with him; he sees the great throne of God richly jewelled, and other thrones, four and twenty round about, upon which sat four and twenty elders.

116.
THE BEASTS
AND THE
ELDERS.

The beasts (borrowed from Ezek. i. 18) full of eyes are there. The lion, the calf, the ox, and the flying eagle.

The beasts we may gather from Ezekiel symbolize the attributes of the Deity—Wisdom, Power, Omniscience, Creation. These are the special agents—the elemental forces of nature, working out the Divine will—whilst the four and twenty elders are the representatives of Humanity.

In the beasts and the elders then, we have the world of Nature and the world of Human Nature personified, both standing in the presence of God.

Innumerable ministering spirits crowd the illimitable avenues of the heavenly perspective. Eternal thunder and lightning rolls and flashes about the jasper and sardine Presence, and the great white throne with its emerald arch; and when the beasts (Elements) rise up to give glory to the Heavenly King, the four and twenty elders (Humanity) cast their crowns down before the throne saying " Thou art worthy, O Lord, to receive glory and honour and power: for Thou hast created all things, and for Thy pleasure they are and were created." Then follows the appearance of a strong angel crying aloud, " Who is worthy to open the Book, and to loose the seals thereof? "

117.
THE STRONG ANGEL.

The Book contains the prophecy of the things which are shortly coming to pass upon the earth. The excitement of the Seer is now raised to the highest pitch, at last he is going to know the future— his inspired longing will be satisfied, and all faithful Christians will be consoled by the spectacle of their foes' confusion, and their own triumph. But alas! no one is found worthy to open the Book, and the prophet weeps because no one is found worthy. Suddenly one steps forward —" A Lamb as it had been slain."

118.
THE BOOK AND THE LAMB.

The favourite sacrificial symbol of the Jews.

The Atonement that lives with God to justify man. The Lamb advances to the Throne, and takes the Book.

At this point the vast expectant assembly is shaken with uncontrollable emotion; from ten thousand times ten thousand voices comes a mighty shout of praise and rapture: " Worthy is the Lamb that was slain to receive power, and riches, and wisdom, and strength, and honour, and glory, and blessing."

"And the four beasts said, Amen. And the four and twenty elders fell down and worshipped Him that liveth for ever and ever."

Throughout the Revelation the cabalistic number of seven is used. There are seven candle-sticks, seven horns, seven eyes, seven spirits of God, seven gifts, seven seals, seven trumpets, seven vials.

119.

AN HISTORIC
RETROSPECT.

The portents about to accompany the vials, the seals, and the trumpets, are indeed somewhat confused. We shall have to go back and re-narrate some events described twice over under the different symbols. This interrupts the flow of the great drama, which is, nevertheless, not without a certain progression, although it is defective in what we should call definite arrangement and literary unity. We shall now be able to cling more or less closely to history. The first seal is opened.

The crowned warrior, on a white horse, who went forth conquering and to conquer, points to the time (63 B.C.) when, under Julius Cæsar in Gaul, and Pompey in Syria, " the whole world " seemed to be converted into so many provinces of Rome.

The great Messianic agitation, the dream of the unearthly deliverer (which Christ fulfilled in the eyes of but a few of His countrymen), began to grow intense from the moment the Jews fell under the Roman sway, and Pompey entered the Holy of Holies, and profaned, without injuring, the temple at Jerusalem.

The second seal is opened. The horseman on the red horse who now appears, is War. He has a great sword, he takes peace from the earth, the people kill each other. Not only war with the Empire, but civil war at Jerusalem. These are the wars of the Cæsars, between I and 66 A.D., when Agrippa had to leave the city, and the *Zealots* and Sadducees killed each other; the massacres

120.
THE RED
HORSE.

throughout Syria and Egypt, which seemed to carry out in the Eastern world the traditions of the Neronian persecution, A.D. 64; the revolt of Vindex, A.D. 68, combined with the revolt at Jerusalem, are evidently the events proper to the warrior on the red horse, with a great sword.

The third seal brings " the black horse, and he that sat on it had a pair of balances in his hand,"

121. THE BLACK HORSE. and a voice cried, "A measure of wheat for a penny, and three measures of barley for a penny; and see thou hurt not the oil and the wine."

This without doubt alludes to the scarcity of provisions at Jerusalem, caused by the people flocking in from all parts of the country, before the devastating march of Vespasian. There was a great scarcity of corn at Rome too in 68.

The fourth seal. The pale horse, and death, and

122. THE PALE HORSE. hell followed him, and " power was given unto them over the fourth part of the earth."

The pale horse—plague and epidemic disease. All the horrors and consequences of protracted war. There may be an allusion to the great plague of 65, in which 30,000 people are said to have died.

The opening of the fifth seal reveals a most touching scene. Beneath the altar are seen the souls of those who were murdered in the gardens of Nero, in 64, where now stand St. Peter's and the Vatican. They are impatient to be avenged — they cry, " How long, O Lord, holy and true, dost Thou not avenge and judge our blood?" and white robes are given unto them, and they are told to wait a little—in fact, the whole vision turns on a series of adjournments.

123.
THE CRY
OF THE
MARTYRS.

With the sixth seal, for a moment, we seem to break into the full crash of the final judgment. The earth quakes, the heavens are rolled together like a scroll—the kings of the earth—the rich—the chief captains tremble—the great day of wrath, the triumph of Messiah seems come; but no, the four angels holding the judgment words are bid to pause.

124.
SILENCE IN
HEAVEN.

As before the last great plague of Egypt, so now before the last doom, the elect must be sealed —the faithful and true of holy Israel, twelve

N

thousand of each tribe, must be sealed and separated from the final wrath.

Out of the midst of this chosen assembly step
forth the white-robed martyrs, who seem to enter
at once into the joy of their Lord. "For the
Lamb which is in the midst of the throne shall
feed them, and shall lead them unto living fountains of waters: and God shall wipe away all tears
from their eyes." Is the end yet? No; there is
silence in heaven for half-an-hour. After this
pause the second act of the great drama begins.

The seventh seal is opened and nothing apparently takes place. An angel steps
forth with a censer full of incense and
fire, and casts the fire upon the earth.

**125.
THE
SEVENTH
SEAL.**

The clouds of incense represent the prayers of
the Saints, who are crying out against their human
persecutors, and these prayers are heard, and are
summed up and answered in the judgment blasts
of the seven trumpets.

Now we have done with the seven seals, and come
to the seven trumpets, in which imagery from
the twelve plagues of Egypt mingles strangely with
the fumes of the Solfatara, the plague of Rome,
and the storms at that time ravaging Asia Minor.

The first trumpet sounds, " and there followed hail and fire mingled with blood, and they were cast upon the earth," alluding to the great storms of 63, 68, and 69 A.D.

The second angel sounded, " and as it were a great mountain burning with fire was cast into the sea," evidently an allusion to the burning mountain of Thera, on an Ægean island, separated from Patmos by a few leagues of sea, but which must have been noticed by the Apostle on his way to or from Rome. At night it might well have seemed a fiery mount cast into the sea, dyeing the waves blood colour (Rev. viii. 8).

" And the third angel sounded, and there fell a great star from heaven," alluding to a fall of meteors, or, perhaps, the appearance of a comet or a fire-ball, not uncommon in seasons of atmospheric disturbance.

With this the prophet associates naïvely the corruption of the waters, reservoirs, or rivers polluted with dead bodies, or foul sewage, fertile source of contagion, as we well know — in short, everywhere the wells were tainted, people were poisoned ; and as there were so many falling stars and celestial signs, the two things were connected together, although they had no real connection, and thus some particular star or comet was singled out and called "Wormwood," because it was supposed to have turned the waters bitter.

And the fourth angel sounded, and the third part of the sun, moon, and stars were smitten. 127. This may allude to one of those THE FALSE eclipses which startled the later years NERO. of Nero, or to the storm of 69 A.D., one of the greatest storms recorded in history.

The ninth chapter records the belief, prevalent at the beginning of A.D. 69, in the almost immediate return of Nero (who died 9th June, 68) from the east—the world could not believe that Nero was dead. When he had committed suicide he was quickly buried; then the false Nero, an impostor, like him in appearance, arose in the island of Cythnos, and the current belief at Ephesus and Patmos was that Nero was making common cause with the east, and especially with the Parthians, whom he had entertained sumptuously at Rome, and that he was about to return.

An invasion of the Parthians was certainly dreaded at Rome in 69 A.D. Through the veil of chapter nine we can still discern the dim outline of these beliefs, and some other curious fragments of Roman contemporary history and local colouring presently to be noted.

The fifth angel sounds, and out of the smoke of a volcanic pit arise clouds of locusts—They darken the sky. Setting aside the evident suggestion of Pharaoh's plagues, it is well-known that after rain-storms the pools of water on volcanic soil are apt to give rise to sudden swarms of locusts, thus the rain, the volcanic soil, and the locusts were naturally associated here.

Any Jew might have noticed the phenomenon, as he landed at Puteoli, and passed near the crater of the Solfatara, and over the smoking phlegrean fields, on his way to Rome. But suddenly the locusts are changed, as in the vision of Joel, into an armed host of light cavalry—"The shapes of the locusts are like unto horses prepared for battle."

The sixth angel (fourteenth verse of ninth chapter) sounds, and a voice says, "Loose the four angels which are bound in the great river Euphrates" (*sic*)—that is, the Eastern nations, especially the Parthians, friends of Nero. Let them come back

128. THE PARTHIANS.

with Nero, to restore for a brief and bloody season the Roman Empire.

Observe, in verse ten, a cryptographic allusion to the Parthian cavalry. The horses are said to be like scorpions, and to have stings in their tails, referring to the famous practice of the Parthian horsemen, who, when pursued after charging, would turn and fly, all the time shooting their arrows behind them—hence the proverb, "Parthian shots."

At the tenth chapter comes another pause—before the opening of the seventh seal. An

129. angel appears and gives the Seer a
THE TEMPLE
MEASURED book, and he swallows it, and the
OFF. taste of it is sweet (an episode evidently borrowed from Jeremiah and Ezekiel, as we at once see by the marginal references in our Bibles). After swallowing the book, which turns bitter, the Seer is further enlightened, and proceeds with the prophecy. The angel then gives him a reed, and tells him to measure the Temple of God.

This was a close reference to what was going on at Jerusalem at the end of 68. Jerusalem was not, in 68, in the hands of the Romans; but it was perfectly clear that the siege that was going on would end in a breach of the walls, and the entry

of the Romans into at least the outer courts of the city and temple ; the rabble of Gentiles that broke into the town at the call of the *Zealots* in 68 may even have invaded the outer court of the temple here (Rev. xi. 2) alluded to; but the Jews never believed that the inner temple itself would be invaded by the Romans—our Lord's prediction to that effect not being generally current till much later—and, therefore, here we find the temple measured off from the rest by the angel's rod :—
" The court which is without the temple leave out, and measure it not, for it is given unto the Gentiles; and the holy city shall they tread under foot forty and two months."

It required no prophet to see that when Vespasian and Titus, the two greatest captains of the age, were drawn up with their armies before the walls of Jerusalem, those walls were doomed. Then there is a description of the scenes in Jerusalem, probably after the slaughter of the Zealots. To what local prophets the two witnesses refer, we cannot at this time tell.

The beast out of the bottomless pit is, of course, Nero redivivus.

But the seventh trumpet is about to sound, and

we might again expect the immediate close. "The kingdoms of this world are become the

130. kingdoms of our Lord, and of His

THE CLOSE Christ; and He shall reign for ever
AGAIN

POSTPONED. and ever."

But at this point, as before, instead of the close, a new series of visions begin to unwind, and we have to go back in order to take in a few more points of contemporary history, before again working up to a climax, thus covering with the seven vials ground already traversed by the seals and the trumpets.

First comes the vision of the "woman clothed with the sun, and the moon under her feet, and upon her head a crown of twelve stars." A man child is born. A red dragon, with seven heads, is ready and eager to swallow up the child that is born. The woman stands for the chosen people of God. The man-child is Jesus Christ, who came from the Jews; the dragon is the Roman power, by whose authority Christ was crucified; but the child is caught up and set at the right hand of God. Then Satan is cast down from heaven, after a great encounter with Michael; and the dragon being baulked of his prey, pursues the woman, that is, persecutes the Judæan Christian church. The woman flees into the wilderness—that is the flight of the Christians A.D. 68, after the massacre by the *Zealots.*

The little community at Pella seems for a time beyond the reach of the dragon, who turns his fury against the other dispersed bodies of Christians throughout Asia Minor. "The dragon was wroth with the woman, and went to make war with the remnant of her seed, which keep the commandments of God, and have the testimony of Jesus Christ."

In the belief of St. John, the world had then about a thousand two hundred and three-score days to run, that is, three years and a-half. Indeed, the general state of the Roman Empire at that time might well give rise to the notion that three years more would be ample time to bring things to a crisis, and wind up human affairs generally.

At chapter xiii. we enter upon a cryptographic vision which clings curiously close to history. A beast rises up out of the sea "having seven heads and ten horns, and upon his horns ten crowns, and upon his heads the name of blasphemy." An exact

131.
THE SEVEN-HEADED BEAST.

historical description of the Roman Empire at the time. Note this: The beast (the Roman power) rose out of the sea, reached the Jews from the Mediterranean, with seven heads and ten horns; the seven heads are the seven Cæsars which had reigned in Rome up to that time— Julius Cæsar, Augustus, Tiberius, Caligula, Claudius, Nero, and Galba—these are the seven heads of the beast. The ten crowned horns or powers were the ten pro-consuls of the Roman Empire, the governors of the Roman Provinces. The name of blasphemy is the title of *Divus*, or *divine*, assumed by the Roman Emperors, and which seemed idolatry to the Jew.

Then in the third verse (chapter xiii.), " And I saw one of his heads, as it were, wounded to death "—a close allusion to history, the rumour of the death of Nero. " And his deadly wound was healed; and all the world wondered after the beast"—that is, the supposed re-appearance of Nero, the actual appearance of a false Nero. He had been wounded, but had recovered ; and then "all the world wondered after the beast," and " they worshipped the dragon which gave power unto the beast"—signifying the adulation, flattery, and actual worship given to the Roman Emperors, especially to Nero. And they said, " who is able to make war with him "; then, " it was given unto him to make war with the Saints, and to overcome them" (persecution of 64) ; " and power was given him over all kindreds, and tongues, and nations." And in the last verse of this chapter read, " Here is wisdom. Let him that hath understanding count the number of the beast: for it is the number of a man ; and his number is six hundred three-score and six." That is how we get at the fact that the beast, representing the Roman power, here means Nero.

It would have laid the Christian writer open to a criminal prosecution had he made this too clear. He veils it in such a way as to be discoverable by those acquainted with the method of Hebrew cryptograph—yet not easily discoverable. The Greek alphabet had a fixed numerical value, but N E R O N K A I S E R will not give 666, but 1005. If the readers tried T E I T A N it would do, and as Titan meant the sun, and Nero-Apollo was a favourite appellation of Nero, that, in default of a better, would help them to identify the beast. But they could do better still if they

132.
THE GREAT
CRYPTOGRAPH
OF NERO.

put N E R O N   K A I S E R into *Hebrew* letters —
נרן קסר $= 50 + 200 + 6 + 50 + 100 + 60 + 200 = 666$,
then you get the solution straight off; and whilst
the description of the beast applies admirably to
Nero, the number of the beast stands revealed as
the number of Nero—and the riddle is solved.

The fourteenth chapter is a little oasis of peace
in the middle of a storm. We see the Lamb
standing on Mount Zion, " and with
Him an hundred forty and four
thousand, having His Father's name
written in their foreheads." In a moment
the spirit of the Seer leaps forward, and
anticipates the calm that shall be, in a peaceful
vision, before it comes. It is the triumph of the
Lord, when the Lamb shall be, surrounded by
those who love Him. We hear no thunders;
nothing at all but the sound of the singers, the
very elect virgins, that follow the Lord in Paradise.

133.

THRUST IN
THY SICKLE.

The scene changes suddenly. The sickle of
God is thrust in, and the earth is reaped—" The
angel thrust in his sickle into the earth, and
gathered the vine of the earth, and cast it into the
great wine - press of the wrath of God." We
might suppose that when the shout that Babylon

is fallen goes forth, and the earth reaped, even now is the end ; but, no.

With the fifteenth chapter comes another post-ponement. Great signs appear in heaven. The seven vials have still to come. "And I saw, as it were, a sea of glass mingled with fire;" and they sing the song of Moses and of the Lamb.

134.
THE SEVEN VIALS.

Then, in the sixteenth chapter, "A great voice out of the temple saying to the seven angels, go your ways, and pour out the vials of the wrath of God upon the earth." Then, in the seven vials, we have repeated much the same as with the seven seals and the seven trumpets. And again is re-peated the story of Nero coming back with his Parthians in the twelfth verse of the sixteenth chapter, "And the sixth angel poured out his vial upon the great river Euphrates"—home of the Eastern allies. This vial evidently corresponds to the sixth trumpet—"And the water thereof was dried up, that the way of the kings of the East might be prepared." Then they are supposed to be gathered together in one place called Armageddon. It is not known what place is here indicated, but it is quite evident that a great battle is now foretold, supposed to be headed on one side by Nero on his recovery and return. We know he never did come back at all, whilst the false Nero was slain in the Spring of 69, a short time after this prophecy was published. The seventh and last vial is poured out; the cities of the nations fall; great Babylon again comes up for judgment; the islands flee away, and the strong angel cries, " It is done."

In the seventeenth chapter the usual interlude occurs, and clings strikingly close to history. " So 135. he carried me away in the spirit into THE SCARLET the wilderness; and I saw a woman sit WOMAN AND THE BEAST. upon a scarlet coloured beast, full of names of blasphemy, having seven heads and ten horns. And the woman was arrayed in purple and scarlet colour," &c. Again we see here the imperial power of Rome, " and upon her forehead was a name written—Mystery, Babylon the great, the mother of harlots, and abominations of the earth."

" The beast that thou sawest was and is not "— that is to say, Nero was alive, then he was wounded to death (" and is not "); but afterwards shall ascend out of the bottomless pit (that is, the

false Nero, as Nero redivivus); but he shall go
into perdition, "and they that dwell on the earth
shall wonder, whose names were not written in
the book of life." Verses nine to thirteen are
very close to history. "Here is the mind which
has wisdom. The seven heads are seven mountains, on which the woman sitteth"—that is, the
seven hills of Rome. "And there are seven
Kings: five are fallen, and one is, and the other
is not yet come." Five are dead, one is, and the
other is not yet come. Here, with that uncertain
and shifting use of chronological order noticed
throughout the Apocalypse, the writer puts himself
back in history a little time. Nero is, and the
other is not yet come. That is, Galba, who was
going to follow him, and had actually followed him
and been assassinated when these words were
written. "And when he cometh he must continue
a short space." Galba only reigned a few months.
And then, "And the beast that was, and is not,
even he is the eighth." Here, as earlier, the
writer parts company with authentic history. Otho
really succeeded Galba, but the prophet supposes
that Nero, not really dead, re-appears, and reigns
for a short time after Galba, thus making the
eighth. This eighth is of the seven, and goeth

into perdition; Nero first standing as the sixth, and hypothetically after Galba as the eighth.

Then the ten horns (the pro-consuls) have one mind, and shall "give their power and strength unto the beast." That is, instead of the Roman Empire collapsing instantly, the generals shall agree to have an Emperor — to establish Nero (*sic*) again. And this last restoration of the head of Rome will make his downfall more tremendous.

In the eighteenth verse, if we desire to know who the scarlet woman is, nothing can be clearer,

136. "And the woman which thou sawest is IMPERIAL that great city (that is, the city of AND PONTIFICAL Rome) which reigneth over the kings of ROME. the earth." Hence, the scarlet woman will do for the Papal Rome by-and-bye, just as well as for the Imperial Rome of those days, for Imperial Rome was succeeded by Papal Rome; and then the enormities of Papal Rome in her worst days are very well fitted by the denunciations applied to the Rome of Nero and Caligula; but of course they really had nothing to do with the Rome of the future, only with the Rome of Peter, and Paul, and John, and Nero.

The judgment very naturally begins with a detailed description of the downfall of the greatest offender—Rome—identified with enmity to Christ by the persecutions of 64. Of course that downfall never took place. Rome was not destroyed. Rome, after the great fire of Nero, was not burnt again within the next few years; but in a few years settled down under a series of wise and powerful Emperors to a long and glorious epoch.

137.
ROME IS
JUDGED.

But now we have to listen to a very different story. A voice cries to the Christians in Rome, "Come out of her my people, that ye be not partakers of her sins, and that ye receive not of her plagues"—that is, come out before the great final destruction; the burning up of the great imperial harlot, by the fires of God. And in the twenty-first verse the prophet says: "And a mighty angel took up a stone like a great mill-stone, and cast it into the sea, saying, Thus with violence shall that great city Babylon be thrown down, and shall be found no more at all." St. John was not, could not have guessed, that in a very few years a series of persecutions would be aimed at the troublesome sect of Christians, under some of the most humane and wise Emperors,

o

such as Hadrian, Trajan, and Marcus Aurelius, and that the Roman Government and order would go on rather more steadily than before.

Rome having been thus summarily cleared out of the way, and utterly demolished in the pro-phetical vision of chapter xviii., the marriage of the Lamb, or final union of Christ with His Church on earth, is prepared. But this is not accomplished without a crowning struggle, for the marriage-feast itself is to consist of the flesh of the vanquished kings, and captains, and horses.

138.

SATAN IS BOUND.

The Word of God—one clothed in a vesture dipped in blood and seated on a white horse—now meets the beast, Nero, and the false prophet, perhaps Simon Magus, in open battle. A great slaughter takes place, and the ringleaders are cast alive into the lake burning with brimstone; in fact, the thermal baths of Baiæ only required a little more heating to become the ready-made fire-and-brimstone lake of the Apocalypse. To the Jew's mind all the volcanic action in the basin of the Mediterranean, and along the Italian and Asian Coasts, was but the preparation for the final judgments depicted in the Apocalypse.

So Rome having first perished, the Roman armies soon succumb, with Nero at their head.

"And the remnant were slain with the sword of him that sat upon the horse, which sword proceeded out of his mouth: and all the fowls were filled with their flesh." We have now arrived at the last postponement. Evil is not all at once annihilated, but Satan is bound for 1,000 years, whilst the martyrs of 64 A.D., and the confessors of Ephesus, or the faithful slain at Jerusalem, rise from their graves, and reign gloriously with Christ for 1,000 years.

Perhaps chapter xiv. has also reference to the Millenium. The reader must judge for himself. At the end of the Millenium a final outburst of evil takes place, and a last great battle. Gog and Magog (from Gogh, mountain, and Magogh, great mountain, spurs of the Caucasus), denoting the Scythian people about the Black and Caspian Seas, are gathered together this time against the Holy City of Jerusalem. They are soon consumed. The great white throne is set. The dead, small and great, stand before God. The devil and all that belong to him are now sent to join the

139.
GOG AND
MAGOG.

O 2

beast and false prophet, and be tormented for ever and ever in the lake which burns with brimstone and fire, and thus the dream of the Jewish hell for the enemies of the Jews is realised. Who would ever have thought to see it pressed for centuries afterwards into the service of the Christian Church?

.

The last judgment is over, the earth has been cleansed. All that offends has been taken away. **140. THE KINGDOM COME AT LAST.** The new heavens and the new earth are ready. The new Jerusalem, city of gems, and light, and glory, is seen descending out of heaven. It is a vision of Oriental splendour. No touch of Greek beauty, no symmetry from Athens, no order or polity from Rome. Simply an impossible and dazzling mass of precious stones, an accumulation of treasure, masses of gold (what the Jew most loved). The eastern mania for magnificence and costliness now runs wild. Twelve gates made out of twelve pearls, streets of gold, walls of jasper. The unartistic mass could only have occurred to a mind devoid of the fine sense of fitness and proportion which has made Greek art immortal, and even opposed to it. At the same time, it is impossible to deny the barbaric splendour of the image thus conjured up, which is still enshrined in the song of Christian peoples—"Jerusalem the golden."

But the prophet reaches the sublime only when he gets away from architecture, about which he knew nothing, to spiritual things, about which he knew so much, "I saw no temple therein: for the Lord God Almighty and the Lamb are the temple of it. And the city had no need of the sun, neither of the moon, to shine in it: for the glory of God did lighten it, and the Lamb is the light thereof. And the gates of it shall not be shut at all by day: for there shall be no night there." The open vision was never more gloriously though sensuously set forth than in these words. With one consent the multitudes of the raised and the living nations now flock towards this sublime centre of the earth. Notice how completely material the whole thing is. How closely it is founded, in spite of Christ's own words, on the Jewish notion of a material kingdom, which the Disciples thought "would presently appear."

The last chapter opens with a vision of peace and refreshment: "And he shewed me a pure river of water of life, clear as crystal, proceeding

141. out of the throne of God and of

THE CRYSTAL the Lamb." But to the end the
RIVER AND
THE TREE OF jealous distinction between Jews and

LIFE. Gentiles is kept up. The fruit of the
tree of life was for the chosen people of God, and
afterwards the Gentiles were favoured. The
Gentiles, although received into the kingdom of
God, were kept at arm's length, only the Jews
have the fruit, the Gentiles may shift with the
leaves of the tree. These are quite good enough
" for the healing of the nations."

The remainder of the chapter is thoroughly
familiar to everyone. At the close, the voices of

142. earth mingle with the voices of

THE SPIRIT heaven, for heaven has indeed at
AND THE
BRIDE. last come down to earth, and the
call to grace and glory is echoed from sphere
to sphere: "The spirit and the bride say,
Come. And let him that is athirst come. And
whosoever will, let him take the water of life
freely." Then follows a curse upon whosoever
adds to, or diminishes from the Apocalypse; and
lastly, the repeated and solemn, but mistaken
declaration, that the prophecy would speedily be

fulfilled: " He which testifieth these things saith, Surely I come quickly. Amen. Even so, come, Lord Jesus."

Thus ends the last, and not the least of those extraordinary prophetical books of the Jews, which together with other fragments of their literature, cover at least 1,500 years of more or less authentic Jewish history, and which are commonly known as the books of the Old and New Testaments.

143.
THE ONE
CLEAR NOTE.

The style and substance of the Revelation unites it to the prophecies of the Old Testament, and to the smaller Apocalypses, such as the fragment, Matthew xxiv., or Jude, of the New. One clear note rings through them all—the indomitable belief that the chosen people of God may suffer, but that ultimately they must conquer.

As far as history goes, this book is a prophecy of things which never did and never can come to pass, since all the people concerned therein have long since faded out, with their interests and policies, and are now but shadowy historical memories;

144.
LETTER AND
SPIRIT.

yet the spiritual teaching of the book will last for ever, for it witnesses to the ineradicable belief in the human breast that, however long evil may endure and seem to conquer, the day must come when the kingdoms of the world will become the kingdoms of our God and of His Christ; when human society shall be purged from evil, and the soul cleansed from sin, and when all those who love His appearing shall enter into the joy of their Lord.

From what has been said we shall readily perceive that throughout the book there is no ground 145. whatever for supposing that any IMMEDIATE portion of it relates to the end of IMPRESSION. this present world, or to any final winding up of the story of the human race.

The immediate impression made by the Apocalypse upon the churches of Asia must have been considerable. The history of the Empire for the next few months seemed to confirm its predictions.

About the 1st February, A.D. 69, the news of Galba's death reached Ephesus—"He was to continue but a short space" (Rev. xvii. 10). Then

followed in rapid succession events which seemed
to threaten the immediate collapse
of the Empire. The accession of
Otho, the persistent claims of Vitellius,
the fall of Otho, the accession of
Vespasian, the battle in the streets of Rome, the
burning of the Capitol; all this could be roughly
but effectively fitted to the vague visions of the
Seer at Patmos. But when Jerusalem fell and the
Jews were for ever dispersed; when the Flavian
dynasty settled down peacefully at Rome, and the
public prosperity began to rise; when Rome,
after persecuting the Christians for some centuries, itself became Christian, and the scarlet
woman herself posed as the great protector and
promoter of Christianity, we can easily see how
profoundly distasteful, both to Greek and Roman
church Doctors, were the bitter denunciations
against Rome and the Roman Government.

With each new persecution of the Christians
the popularity of the Revelation had revived; but
a time came when its Jewish theology, and its
hatred of the Nicolaitanes did not square with
the triumph of the liberal Christianity and
the Pauline theology, and when moreover the
prophecies were seen to be clearly unfulfilled.

146.
WHY
REVELATION
LOST
GROUND.

A future had, therefore, to be created for a work so undoubtedly early and probably authentic

147.
HOW
REVELATION
REGAINED
ITS PLACE.

as the Revelation ; though we can hardly wonder at the unwillingness of the Latin Doctors to attribute to an Apostle sentiments in opposition to the sense of the cultivated Gentile world, to which they chiefly belonged, we can also appreciate the intense aversion which Eastern Christians (who had imbibed Greek culture) would naturally have to Jewish Millenarianism, and anything else Jewish—so what with Romans and what with Greeks it was rather difficult to know what should be done with the Apocalypse.

The Eastern church, indeed, went so far as to declare the book altogether Apocryphal, a view not shared by the Western church; yet it was not really re-instated in the popular affections until Joachim de Flore, in the twelfth century, casting to the winds the tradition of the Fathers, boldly extended the fulfilment of the Apocalypse beyond the modest limit of three years, which it claims for itself, to the unnumbered ages which must precede some future coming of Christ to earth, and some future last judgment.

This bold speculation struck the keynote of all

those wild interpretations which have since been fitted on to the signs of the times; and which will continue to be fitted on to the elastic statements and images of the Apocalypse, as long as people steadily refuse to read Tacitus and Suetonius by the side of St. John; as long, in short, as people will not study the New Testament intelligently by the light of its contemporary history, so long will they be the prey of those commentators who are ingenious without being intelligent, and who seem able to do nothing with the contemporary history—except twist it.

NOVELLO, EWER & Co., Printers, 69 & 70, Dean Street, Soho, London, W

WORKS BY THE REV. H. R. HAWEIS, M.A.

THEOLOGICAL.

CHRIST AND CHRISTIANITY. In Five Vols.

THE STORY OF THE FOUR.	
(Evangelists.)	*Now Ready.*
THE PICTURE OF JESUS.	
(The Master.)	*In November.*
THE PICTURE OF PAUL.	
(The Disciple.)	*In February.*
THE CONQUERING CROSS.	
(The Church.)	*At Easter.*
THE LIGHT OF THE NATIONS.	
(Asia, Africa, Europe.)	*In May.*

Published by CHARLES BURNET & CO.,
9, Buckingham Street, Strand.

THOUGHTS FOR THE TIMES. Thirteenth Edition.

SPEECH IN SEASON. Sixth Edition.

CURRENT COIN. Sixth Edition.

ARROWS IN THE AIR. Sixth Edition.

POETS IN THE PULPIT. Fourth Edition.

THE KEY FOR 1884. Fifteenth Thousand. 1s.

WINGED WORDS.

UNSECTARIAN FAMILY PRAYERS. New and cheaper Edition.

SECULAR.

MUSIC AND MORALS. Fourteenth Edition.

MY MUSICAL LIFE. Second Edition.

AMERICAN HUMORISTS. Second Edition.

ASHES TO ASHES. Second Edition.

PET; OR, PASTIMES AND PENALTIES. Third Edition.

Sold by JOHN BUMPUS, 350, Oxford Street
and by all Booksellers.